THE LITTLE BOOK OF LUNCH

THE LITTLE BOOK OF LUNCH

100 RECIPES & IDEAS TO RECLAIM THE LUNCH HOUR

CAROLINE CRAIG AND SOPHIE MISSING

Regan Arts.

NEW YORK

Regan Arts.

Regan Arts
65 Bleecker Street
New York, NY 10012

First published by Square Peg, a division of The Random House Group Ltd

First Regan Arts hardcover edition May 2015.

Library of Congress Control Number: 2014955542

ISBN 978-1-941393-22-2

Designed by Secondary Modern
Photography by David Loftus, except pg. 21: ©Sukiyaki/Shutterstock
Food and prop styling by Sophie Missing and Caroline Craig
Jacket design by Richard Ljoenes

Printed in China.

10 9 8 7 6 5 4 3 2 1

*"When people you greatly admire appear to be thinking deep thoughts,
they probably are thinking about lunch."*
Douglas Adams

*"A man may be a pessimistic determinist before lunch
and an optimistic believer in the will's freedom after it."*
Aldous Huxley

*"It is more fun to talk with someone who doesn't use long, difficult words
but rather short, easy words like 'What about lunch?'"*
Winnie the Pooh

GREAT IDEAS
(plus some others)

AUTO-PENCIL

CONTENTS

LUNCH: A MANIFESTO

*L*unch, *that oft-overlooked middleman between breakfast and dinner, is, let's be honest, the highlight of the working day. Whether you're a worker or a student, who doesn't furtively glance at the time on a weekday morning, mentally urging the little numbers to reach a socially acceptable hour for respite, and a killer sandwich? We definitely do. In fact, our shared love of the lunch hour—and a really, really great bacon and avocado sandwich (see page 56) consumed before the technically acceptable lunching hour on a frosty train into the city (trains, like planes, exist beyond the zones of time, especially when en route to a company sales conference)—is how The Little Book of Lunch came about.*

This book is filled with delicious and simple recipes for the working person's packed lunch box, for food lovers who have run out of steam and inspiration, and for anyone in a rut who is tired of spending a large chunk of their wages on the same old thing week after week. Follow these recipes and tips and it won't be long before you are savoring the comforting goodness of a homemade lunch, cheered and reassured by the knowledge that you know exactly what went into it and that it is made precisely to your taste.

But back to the beginning. We're all busy people. So, why bother with the extra fuss? The simple answer is that lunch—especially while you are at work, *working*—is one of life's great pleasures, yet one that is easily overlooked. It's pretty common for most people to spend as little time and effort as possible on lunch because a) they're too busy to stop, and b) they want to cram as much into their working day as possible before packing up and sprinting home to begin real life. It's a difficult

pattern to break, but the truth is that life doesn't begin at the weekend, or at 6:30 p.m. on a weekday. This is your life, and, small-fry though it may seem, having a lunch that you have made yourself to look forward to, can improve it. Face it, if you've bought a limp egg salad sandwich from the nearest deli, we're not surprised that you want to inhale it, then pretend it never happened. But if you have lovingly put together your lunch, chances are you're going to want to take some time to savor it.

Our extensive scientific research[1] has shown that a proper meal—and a proper break—really can turn your day around. And even your employers, were they to speak of such trivial things, would concede that distance, both physical and metaphorical, leads to more productive thinking. Yes, this hour is yours to have and yours for the taking.

So, taking a break is good. But what do you eat during it, especially when you're

1 *Well, working in a series of stores and offices for the last few years.*

pushed for time as it is? For the city dweller, there have never been more options. Sandwiches, soups, salads, or sushi: the choices are overwhelming. Yet, as more convenience chains open, catering to our every fancy and fad, the less satisfaction we seem to get from popping out for that hot wrap or grabbing that bite to eat. Why? Because, although it sounds ridiculous, once the novelty has worn off, it often feels like no one is selling anything you actually want to eat. Most people have their standby lunch item, but there's something a bit depressing about wearily buying the same sandwich day in, day out, and getting excited when a new soup is added to your favorite deli's menu, if only because it promises to mix things up a bit. Plus, shelling out for your lunch every day is *expensive*. Even if you play it safe (cheese and tomato) and don't go wild (artisan baguette), add a drink and a coffee and we conservatively estimate that you will spend at least $50 a week on your lunch—that's over $2,500 a year!

Of course, not everyone buys their lunch—far from it. There are many people who, not working on a street with three Pret A Mangers within five minutes walk, bring in a packed lunch every day. But it's still easy to fall into the same trap of routine, as even those with the best intentions can lose enthusiasm for homemade lunching after transfering chili con carne batch number thirty-three of the year into a Tupperware container that has seen better days. Which is where we come in. We know the pain of waking up late with only twenty minutes in which to wash, dress ourselves in respectable garb, *and* try to make something palatable for our lunch, especially after looking in the fridge and seeing one slice of Velveeta and two eggs. *The Little Book of Lunch* is the result of our hard-won wisdom. We hope these recipes and tips will inspire you to enjoy a piece of home in the midst of work's microcosmic chaos, save some money, and not settle for whatever dregs are left on the shop shelves after the 12:30 p.m. stampede. It might not always be practical or convenient (if you have a killer hangover, you are unlikely to care about making sure your salad is evenly dressed—in fact, it's unlikely you'll be eating salad at all) to make yourself lunch every day, but the lunch hour should be something greater than a store-bought sandwich bolted down while hunched over your keyboard.

Even if you only do it once a week, opening a lunch box, dressing a home-made salad at work, or unwrapping a foil parcel from home will make you feel a sense of pride and even a shiver of smugness as your colleagues glance over in envy. And surely this alone makes it worth taking a break and reclaiming the lunch hour.

PACKED LUNCH ESSENTIALS: Choosing your Receptacle

PACKED LUNCH ESSENTIALS

CHOOSING YOUR RECEPTACLE
THE LUNCH BOX CARRIER

A scrunched up plastic bag is a classic lunch conveyer. If it ain't broke, why fix it? you may ask, but, dear lunch eater, there are other options. And, if you have decided to put some effort into making your lunch, why not flaunt it?

The executive sandwich carrier
Meaning that briefcase you bought at your local thrift store that you never use. Now that everyone's gone paperless you will find that it is perfect for holding an apple, a tenderly wrapped sandwich, and your journal of choice. Swing it jauntily.

The retro tin
Yup, that Felix the Cat/Teenage Mutant Ninja Turtles tin box from first grade, with your name and address taped to the inside, is actually useful again. And quite cool, in a slightly regressive way.

The brown paper bag
Minimalism at its most chic, the brown paper bag suggests that you bought your lunch at a famous New York deli. Buy in bulk online, and start a brown paper bag lunch gang.

The eco-friendly cotton tote
Available pretty much anywhere, often for free. Save the planet and hide your plastic-bag-encased Tupperware at the same time.

The picnic basket
A vintage classic. For the sartorially brave.

The right receptacle obviously depends on the lunch you have chosen to make. Some recipes require assembly just before eating, with different components needing to be packed separately. The main thing you can do to help you on your packed-lunch endeavors is to purchase containers in lots of different sizes. But, as with all accessories, some are more attractive than others.

The enamel lunch pail
The Chanel handbag of lunch containers: expensive but excellent quality, and will never date. Etsy.com has an excellent selection.

The tiffin tin
Scour eBay for a genuine vintage floral painted beauty, or find an updated stainless steel version at most department stores. Embark upon your commute safe in the knowledge that your bread and salad are safely enclosed in separate metal compartments.

Thermos
Handy for the dismal al desko lunch when you're superglued to your seat. If your place of work doesn't have a microwave, you'll need one of these to enjoy the soups in this book. More on these later.

Tupperware
A bit like a Volvo. Not particularly pretty, but safe and reliable; you know your pasta salad is in good hands. You can also transport soup in them with confidence. One should set aside at least three for packed lunch purposes: a large one for things like lettuce, which takes up lots of room and mustn't be squashed en route; a medium-size one, which can be used

for most concoctions, and crucially, a miniature one to house salad dressing, which can be nestled in either of the aforementioned, like a Russian doll.

IMPROVISING

So not everyone is going to be fussed about hunting down a utilitarian imitation WW2 mess tin to house their quinoa or spending a small fortune on enamelware. We understand. Thankfully there are other options and household items you can requisition to great effect.

The super-sized pickle jar
Fill it up with your packed lunch and get a free workout as you lug it on the commute.

The mini jam jar
A B&B staple, these little beauties are perfect for housing your salad dressing.

The quart-sized plastic ice cream box
Conveniently sized and often with gloriously retro packaging: do you need another excuse to buy some gelato or vanilla ice cream?

PACK IT UP, PACK IT IN

THE WELL-STOCKED HOME
EQUIPMENT

You may now be the proud owner of a fine selection of receptacles, but you still need a few more things to make sure that your lunch gets from A to B in optimum condition. Aluminum foil seems to be one of those household items that no one remembers to replace, but parchment paper is a fine substitute for wrapping a sandwich and looks incredibly pleasing when secured with a piece of plain string. Look at what you already have around you: we wrap bread rolls and boiled eggs in clean dish towels when we've run out of Tupperware, or transport washed salad in plastic bags. All very specialist, you'll agree.

This is what you will need to ensure total lunch readiness, at all times:

• Parchment paper
• Aluminum foil
• Plastic wrap
• String
• Clean dish towels
• Hand blender, for puréeing soups and
making dips and fancy dressings;
a kitchen essential

There is no denying that having the ingredients for a delicious packed lunch is a combination of timing, logistics, and preparation. By *preparation* we don't necessarily mean preparing seven lunches on a Sunday night. What we mean is getting into the habit of buying key items, which will ensure that you will always be able to rustle up quick and tasty lunches.

We've all opened the kitchen cabinet and stared blankly into the abyss, feeling a total lack of inspiration at the half packet of spaghetti and can of red salmon that's been there for two years, then shut the door and resigned ourselves to buying yet another overpriced tuna mayo baguette. Keep a well-stocked kitchen, and this needn't be the case.

These are the ingredients that we find ourselves coming back to, and that we would recommend buying and replenishing:

- Anchovies
(if you're buying small cans and only need a few for a recipe, freeze the remainder)
- Avocados
- Capers
- Carrots
- Cherry tomatoes
(these can keep for a week or so in a little bowl on the counter—don't store them in the fridge)
- Chorizo (buy whole sausages from your local deli or supermarket)
- Couscous
- Dried chili flakes
- Dried pasta—stock a variety of shapes to suit your mood

- Eggs
- Fresh cilantro
- Frozen ready-to-bake baguettes
- Frozen peas
- Fruit
- Green and black olives (in jars)
- Lemons and limes
- Pita bread (store in the freezer)
- Red onions and scallions
- Canned beans: cannellini, pinto
- Canned chickpeas
- Canned tomatoes
- Canned tuna

No sense beating about the bush here: herbs are something we feel strongly about, as they lift dishes to new heights. Just keep those godforsaken store-bought herb pots alive. How often have you looked at the ingredients required for a recipe from a cookbook and felt your heart sink at the list of three "oh so convenient" handfuls of different fresh herbs? As if. At a minimum of $3 a bunch, these herbs can cost as much as a decent steak when put together. Cue penury.

We've done our utmost to keep costs down and have identified the herbs that are easiest to keep on life support: basil, mint, and rosemary. You don't need a garden—we grow ours on our windowsills, and having even the tiniest of pots will save you both money and resentment (reserve that anger for your commute or arrival at work, like normal people) when a recipe calls for yet another bunch of delicious, ruinous herbs.

Invest in a small bag of compost and repot your herbs so that their roots have enough room to grow. Place them by a window and water them every other morning (try not to drown them—plants, like people, can have too much love). We're not green-fingered by any means, but we've been able to keep ours alive. Even the casualties (RIP young Basil the First) have lasted for at least six to eight weeks at a time. Not bad for a $3.50 pot from the supermarket.

A fresh herb garden is the ideal, but that is obviously not going to be a reality if you live in a dark basement apartment. So, if and when when you do buy cut herbs, systematically remove the packaging when you get home and follow this conservation trick: take a clean dish towel and run it under the cold tap to wet it completely. Squeeze out the excess water, wrap your herbs in it and store in the fridge drawer. You will be amazed at how long they keep—even softer herbs. Supermarkets don't tell you this on the packaging because they want you to keep buying them again and again.

A final note in this lengthy herb discussion: if you don't have all of the herb ingredients for a recipe, do not despair. If a recipe calls for a specific combination and you only have, say, basil, just make it anyway with what you've got. You never know, you might find a new delicious combination.

Whether you're a teacher, office worker, or truck driver, your workspace is your little home away from home, adorned with cheering postcards, photographs, and maybe even a stress ball. And if it can take this junk, why not a cheeky couple of small bottles of oil and vinegar too? If you are lucky enough to have access to a kitchen in which you can store foodstuff without having to resort to the use of passive-aggressive Post-its [Jeff's—please DO NOT TOUCH :)], then of course you don't need to clutter your immediate work zone, but if not, do not despair. You don't need much to ensure you have a full desk survival kit at the ready.

Seasoning

There's nothing more annoying than munching on something accidentally underseasoned with no means of doing anything about it. If you don't keep a stash of salt and pepper at your desk, get into the habit of bringing some in from home, wrapped in little squares of folded paper or foil. This also works well for any extra dried ingredients you might want to bring, like chili flakes or basil.

Dressing

Salad, be it leaf- or grain-based, should be coated in its dressing moments before eating. If you dress it in the morning before you leave the house, then it will be a soggy, decaying mess come lunchtime, and all your efforts will have been in vain. Pack your dressing separately and bring it with you.

As we've already mentioned, you don't have to buy a special container: mini jam or pickle jars are perfect for making and transporting dressing. Just make sure that you give them a good clean before use, fasten the lid very tightly, and pack them inside the salad container to further minimize the chance of any leakage.

Alternatively, if you have the space, keeping dressing ingredients at work will save you having to make some in the morning and will gain you a little precious time.

These are the essentials that we would recommend keeping within easy reach in the workplace. Your colleagues may initially think you're a weirdo, but it's only a matter of time before your desk buddy asks for a pinch of salt or a splash of balsamic vinegar to enliven their sad salad.

• Salt
• Pepper
• Extra-virgin olive oil
• Vinegar
• Chili sauce (Sriracha chili sauce is an excellent desk condiment as it doesn't need refrigeration)
• Napkins
• Wet wipes (for greasy keyboards)
• A penknife (keep in your locked desk drawer before Health and Safety come knocking)
• A variety of sauces (collect packets from takeout restaurants and sandwich chains)

A NOTE ON SIDES

This is a recipe book full of main courses for lunch. Where appropriate, we've suggested lovely sides: for example a little crunchy cucumber to go with the Moroccan spinach (see page 41), or a piece of crusty bread to go with your Leek soup (see page 36). However, it is up to you to balance the rest of your meal. Don't forget that nature has already created the most perfect, transportable, delicious packed lunch items encased in biodegradable packaging: fruit. Bring some with you every single day. There is no denying that vegetables form a huge part of the recipes in this book. The reason for this is quite simple: meat is best enjoyed as soon as it's cooked. The longer you leave it, the tougher it gets. Not exactly conducive to picnic lunches, eh?

1: WHOLESOME AND HEALTHY

WHEN YOU NEED SOMETHING GREEN AND CRUNCHY AND FRESH

We've all been there: Monday morning, a general sense that you have pickled parts of your body over the weekend and the realization that you've eaten enough beige food to sink a battleship and drunk enough booze to float it. With as many vitamin combinations as possible, and more emphasis on the "lite" than the junk, this chapter will provide you with a much-needed injection of vitality (and stop you fainting at the sight of another chip).

If you're keeping an eye on your waistline, the workplace can be a surprisingly suitable battleground, and the homemade lunch a marvelous exercise in portion control. Think of it this way: you are at least two miles from your kitchen fridge, so snacking or "seconds" is out of the question. You can *only* eat what you packed that morning. (If you can resist the packet of milk chocolates your boss purchased as a team morale booster.)

SALAD NIÇOISE
WITH A BOILED EGG IN ITS SHELL

Preparation time: 15 minutes. Makes 1 serving

- 7 baby romaine lettuce leaves
- 4 plum or cherry tomatoes
- 2 in piece of cucumber, sliced into chunks
- 1 egg
- small handful of green beans, ends cut
- 4 anchovies
- 6 black olives

For the dressing
- 1 tbsp extra-virgin olive oil
- salt and freshly ground black pepper
- ½ small garlic clove, crushed
- 1 tsp Dijon mustard
- 1 tsp red wine vinegar

This is such a classic, simple salad, but it's not thought of as particularly portable because of its slightly soggy ingredients. No one wants to eat an egg that has been sliced and hanging around next to some lettuce leaves since 8 a.m., but if you leave it in its shell then, come lunchtime, the yolk will be golden, intact, and still slightly soft. Perfect.

Fill a small pan with water and place over a high heat. Wash and dry the lettuce, tomatoes, and cucumber and place in your lunch container (we recommend using a large, spacious one in this instance). Once the water is boiling, gently add the egg. Set your watch/oven timer/phone for 7 minutes if you like a softer yolk, 8 minutes if you like a firmer set yolk. After 2 minutes, spoon your green beans into the same boiling water and blanch them alongside the egg for a couple of minutes or until you are happy with how cooked they are (we like ours crunchy), then remove from the pan and refresh under cold water. Add all the dressing ingredients to a mini jam jar and shake. Place the anchovies and olives in another empty jar (or similar appropriately sized container) and shut securely.

Take the egg off the heat as soon as the time is up, drain away the hot water, and leave to stand in a bowl of cold water for 5 minutes.

Pat dry the green beans and add to the rest of the salad. Dry off the boiled egg: it should be cool now, so you can nestle it in the salad.

Come lunchtime
Assemble your salad by arranging everything on a plate (or in your container). Place the anchovies and olives on top. Crack and peel your egg, and cut into quarters. Finally, pour over the dressing and enjoy.

AVOCADO SALAD

Preparation time: 5 minutes
Makes 1 serving

- *handful of washed baby romaine leaves, or another crunchy lettuce*
- *6 cherry tomatoes (or 1 regular tomato)*
- *2½ in piece of cucumber*
- *½ ripe avocado (wrap the remaining half in plastic wrap and keep in the fridge)*
- *squeeze of lemon or lime juice*
- *1 flatbread wrap, or pita*

For the dressing
- *2 tsp crème fraîche*
- *squeeze of lemon juice*
- *tiny splash of cider or white wine vinegar*
- *sea salt*

It's amazing how lettuce, tomato, and cucumber can become something quite special with the addition of avocado and a creamy dressing. Healthy too. This is especially nice as a pita filling or on a flatbread: make sure you add the dressing just before eating, so your salad doesn't get soggy.

Add a large fistful of washed and dried crunchy lettuce leaves (we find a peppery leaf like arugula too overpowering here; the avocado is the star of the show) to your container. Slice the tomatoes and cucumber and add to the leaves. Squeeze a little lemon juice over the avocado half, cover with plastic wrap and store with the rest of your salad.

For the dressing, mix together the crème fraîche, lemon juice, vinegar, and salt. Store in a tightly sealed mini container and nestle into your larger salad container.

Come lunchtime
Using a teaspoon, spoon out the avocado and mix with your salad, taking care not to smush it too much. Pour over your dressing and enjoy in a wrap, or tucked into a pita.

If you're feeling fancy and have the time, lightly toasted pine nuts are a nice addition. Simply heat a frying pan until hot, then dry-fry a small handful until golden. When cool, sprinkle over the salad.

If you're looking for inspiration for that spare half avocado (which will admittedly have a limited fridge life), why not eat it for breakfast the following morning on a piece of toast, with a sprinkling of salt, a few chili flakes, and a squeeze of lemon? Delicious. Also works well on toasted split whole wheat pita as a quick and easy lunchtime snack.

WHOLESOME AND HEALTHY: *Salads for well-meaning Mondays*

TABOULEH

Preparation time: 15 minutes
Makes 1 serving

- 2 oz couscous
- ½ small red onion, finely chopped
- 2 medium-sized tomatoes, finely chopped
- 3 in piece of cucumber, finely chopped
- large handful of mint leaves, stalks removed
- large handful of flat-leaf parsley, stalks removed
- slice of lemon

For the dressing
- ½ garlic clove, crushed
- juice of ½ lemon
- salt and freshly ground black pepper
- 2 tbsp extra-virgin olive oil

Tabouleh can be enjoyed all year round and, apart from the couscous, involves zero cooking, earning this delicious Moroccan version bonus lunch points. It also keeps for days in the fridge should you decide to make more than one batch.

Open a lunch pail and cover the base with a layer of couscous grains. Pour freshly boiled water into the pail until the couscous is completely covered, with a little extra water on top. Leave to absorb for a few minutes under a dish towel before separating the grains with a fork and leaving to cool.

Meanwhile, prepare the red onion, tomatoes, cucumber, and herbs. It is best to add these to completely cooled and forked couscous, so now would probably be an ideal time to get dressed or have breakfast.

When you are ready to leave for work, add the herbs and chopped vegetables to the couscous, along with the dressing ingredients. Mix and top with a slice of lemon, in case you want to adjust the seasoning at lunchtime. Close the pail and journey to work, popping it in the fridge on arrival, if possible.

TIP FOR BULKING UP
If you need something more filling, try packing a toasted pita with the prepared tabouleh. Transport the pita to work wrapped in foil or brown paper with the dressing in a separate container. When you're ready to eat, stuff the pita with the salad before drizzling the garlicky dressing over the contents. If you really want to treat yourself, add some crumbled feta cheese for a tangy hit.

CHICKPEA, PARMESAN & RED ONION SALAD

....

Preparation time: 12 minutes
Makes 1 serving

- *handful of green beans, ends cut*
- *½ x 15 oz can chickpeas*
- *1 tbsp grated Parmesan*
- *½ red onion, thinly sliced*
- *handful of cherry tomatoes*
- *small handful of fresh basil*
- *Smoked herring (if you don't have a fridge at work, omit the herring)*

For the dressing
- *1 tbsp extra-virgin olive oil*
- *1 tsp red wine vinegar*
- *generous pinch of salt and freshly ground black pepper*

....

Chickpeas really are a star lunch ingredient: open, drain, and practically-hey-presto-lunch. We would recommend experimenting with different brands as there is a lot of variation in taste among them. Goya or Pastene are nice. For this recipe, we find a whole can is too much for just one person but not quite enough for two, so you could use any leftover chickpeas the following day in the Rainbow rescue salad (see page 31). This is a lovely, refreshing, and filling salad, with Parmesan and chickpeas the firmest of friends.

....

Bring a pan of salted water to a boil. Once the water is bubbling, add the green beans and blanch for 4 minutes.

Meanwhile, drain the chickpeas and place half the contents at the bottom of a two-tiered lunch pail or tiffin tin. Grate over the Parmesan and stir in the sliced onion. When the green beans are ready, drain and run them under a cold tap to cool (you don't want to pack them too hot). Pat dry using a paper towel and add them to the lunch pail along with the whole cherry tomatoes. Pop some basil leaves on top. The herring should be kept separate until you are ready to eat, so add it to the top tier of the tiffin tin, or pack in a separate container.

Add the dressing ingredients to a mini container and nestle into your salad tin. Make your way to work, and pop the pail in the fridge on arrival.

Come lunchtime
Remove from the fridge just before eating and transfer the mixture onto a plate. Use a fork to separate the fish into flakes and discard the skin. You can also, if you wish, cut the cherry tomatoes in half. Shake the dressing, pour it over the salad, and mix gently. Admire the beautiful colors, and feast.

WHOLESOME AND HEALTHY: Salads for well-meaning Mondays

RAINBOW RESCUE
YOUR FIVE-A-DAY IN A SINGLE JAR

....

Preparation time: 10 minutes
Makes 1 serving

- *½ x 15 oz can chickpeas*
- *¼ small red cabbage, thinly sliced*
- *½ red onion, thinly sliced*
- *1 carrot, grated*
- *3 in piece of cucumber, diced*
- *1 tomato, diced*
- *handful of arugula or fresh spinach*

For the dressing
- *juice of 1 lime*
- *1 tbsp white wine vinegar*
- *splash of soy sauce*
- *splash of fish sauce*
- *salt and freshly ground black pepper*
- *pinch of superfine sugar*

....

In the morning

Open the can of chickpeas and drain. Pop half in a bowl in the fridge and use the following day (see page 29). In a large container or jar, line the bottom with the chickpeas. For the next layer add enough sliced red cabbage to cover. Follow with the sliced red onion and grated carrot. Finally, add the diced cucumber and tomato. Top it off with the spinach or arugula leaves. To make the dressing mix all the ingredients together in a small jam jar.

Come lunchtime

Give the dressing jar a good shake before drizzling over your salad.

HERBY QUINOA WITH PEAS
& SEASONAL GREENS

Preparation time: 25 minutes
Makes 1 serving

- 1 portion of quinoa
- handful of asparagus
(woody ends cut off)
- 3 tbsp frozen peas
- 1 tbsp freshly chopped cilantro
- 1 tbsp freshly chopped mint
- 1 tbsp freshly chopped basil

For the dressing
- juice of ½ lemon
- 2–3 tsp extra-virgin olive oil
- salt and freshly ground black pepper

Quinoa is both a delicious and filling ingredient, thanks to its protein content, and is now readily available in most supermarkets. It takes a little longer to cook than other grains, so if you are short of time make it the night before or substitute with couscous. Asparagus is our preferred vegetable for this dish, but if it's the wrong time of year, cooked green beans are just as good.

The night before
Cook the quinoa according to the package instructions. Drain and leave to cool before popping in your lunch pail or container and leaving in the fridge overnight.

In the morning
Put a large pan filled with an inch of salted water on the heat. Once the water is bubbling, add the asparagus and simmer, lid on, for about 3 minutes. Thirty seconds before you're due to remove the pan from the heat, add the peas. When the time is up, drain in a colander and run it all under the cold tap.

Once cool, extract the asparagus from the colander and chop into bite-sized

pieces. Add to the quinoa in your container along with the peas and chopped herbs. Your lunch is almost ready.

Finally, add the dressing ingredients to a very small container—as usual, ideally compact enough to fit *inside* your lunch pail amongst the herby quinoa, for convenience. Tightly close all the lids and skip along the streets to work.

Come lunchtime
Give the dressing container a good shake and pour over the quinoa, stirring well to coat evenly. Adjust the seasoning if necessary, and enjoy!

WHOLESOME AND HEALTHY: *Simple and soothing*

SPEEDY COUSCOUS VARIATION

If you're in a real rush to prepare this, use couscous instead of quinoa and simply stir in "raw" peas (frozen or fresh), omitting the cooked asparagus. Just as delicious and takes about 3 minutes. For this super speedy version in the morning, add a few tablespoons of couscous grains directly into your lunch pail, and just cover with boiling water and a dish towel. Once the grains are plump and fluffy, use a fork to separate them, then stir in a cupful of frozen peas, along with the chopped herbs. The genius of peas is that, like carrots, you do not have to cook them: the peas gently defrost in the warm couscous and are perfectly ready to eat come lunchtime. Drizzle over some olive oil, salt, and a squeeze of lemon, and you're all set.

FENNEL WITH LEMON CHICKEN

Preparation time: 12 minutes
Makes 1 serving

- 1 boneless skinless chicken breast
- zest of ⅓ lemon, plus a squeeze of lemon juice
- freshly ground black pepper
- 1 tsp extra-virgin olive oil
- 1 fennel bulb
- few crunchy lettuce leaves, e.g., baby romaine

- 1 tsp slivered almonds (optional)
- sprinkling of freshly chopped thyme, flat-leaf parsley, or basil (optional)

For the dressing
- 1½ tsp extra-virgin olive oil
- generous pinch of salt

A tart and refreshing dish, also nice with leftover rice. If you want to keep it carb-free, enjoy as is.

Thinly slice the chicken breast and place in a bowl. Put a frying (or griddle) pan on a medium heat. Add the lemon zest, black pepper, olive oil, and lemon juice to the bowl and stir until evenly coated. Pour everything into the hot pan, lowering the heat if the sizzling sound on impact is too wild: you don't want to be late for work, but you certainly don't want to frazzle your chicken.

While the chicken is cooking, prepare your lunch receptacle: trim and then finely slice or grate in the fennel. Roughly chop your lettuce and add to the container. Top with the slivered almonds if using. The chicken should be almost ready and looking nicely golden. Add whatever green herb you're using now. If the chicken needs a few more minutes, take this opportunity to make your little

dressing: add the ingredients to either a miniature jam jar or small Tupperware container. Turn the heat off and leave the chicken to cool on the upturned lid of your lunch receptacle (at this stage, we sometimes grind some fancy salt over it).

Now would be a good time to get ready for work.

When you're ready to leave, top the fennel salad with the slightly cooled chicken, along with the lemony juices from the pan. Consider storing in the fridge at work, but remove an hour before eating.

Come lunchtime
The juices will have softened the fennel and lettuce. When you're about to eat, pour over the dressing and give it a good stir to coat evenly.

LEEK SOUP

Preparation time: 10 minutes, plus 15–20 minutes cooking
Makes 3 servings

- 1½ lbs leeks
- 1 tbsp extra-virgin olive oil and 1 tsp butter
- salt and freshly ground black pepper

This is the classic, the home broth, the re-invigorator. Designed to absolve you from your food sins. It is also suitable for freezing. We often make this in the morning, but it can of course be made the night before. We like our soups thick and rustic, so if you prefer yours a little runnier, simply increase the quantity of water used.

Trim both ends of the leeks and score them in the middle, right down their length, fanning them open under a running tap to remove any grit. Slice the leeks into little circles, half an inch thick. Drizzle the olive oil and butter into a large, heavy-bottomed pan and place on the stove on a medium heat. Fill a small pot or saucepan with 6 cups fresh water and put on to boil. Add the leeks to the pan and toss in the oil to coat evenly. Sprinkle over a generous amount of black pepper and mix again. Pop a lid on the pan and leave to steam for a few minutes while the water boils.

Lift the lid off and have a glance at the leeks: they should be soft and shiny. Give them a stir and leave to steam in their juices for a bit longer if they need it, making sure they don't catch at the bottom of the pan (add a splash or two of water if they do).

When the water has boiled, add it to the leek pan along with plenty of salt and bring to a boil. Then immediately lower the heat and leave to simmer, uncovered. Jump in the shower.

After 15 minutes, turn off the heat and leave to cool for a few minutes before puréeing with a hand blender. Immediately transfer into your thermos, or if making the night before, pop a lid on. Leave overnight on the stove and reheat in the morning before leaving for work.

A WORD OF CAUTION
Although seemingly innocuous, leeks are part of the strong-smelling onion family, so perhaps a desk lunch is best avoided in this instance.

VIETNAMESE SALAD

Preparation time: 15 minutes of serious veg chopping—if you want to save some time, peel or grate the carrot instead of chopping, as this is the most time-consuming bit and can be painful on the wrists.
Makes 2 servings (if you are feeling generous)

- ⅛ white or red cabbage, sliced into thin strips
- 1 carrot, peeled and finely chopped into matchsticks
- 2 scallions, finely chopped
- 4 radishes, sliced
- 6 cherry or small plum tomatoes, quartered
- 4 leaves baby romaine or iceberg lettuce, shredded
- handful of shredded leftover chicken (optional)
- large handful of mint, leaves picked and washed

- large handful of cilantro, leaves picked and washed

For the dressing
- 1 small red chili, seeded and chopped
- 3 tbsp rice wine vinegar
- 1 tbsp fish sauce
- 1 tsp sweet chili sauce
- juice of ½ lime
- pinch of salt
- 1 tsp sugar

There is something so refreshing about a Vietnamese salad, with its combination of crunchy raw veg and brain-awakening dressing. It's just the thing for the sort of day when you stayed out for one too many post-work drinks the night before and want something healthier than a coma-inducing baked potato with a side of fries. Ready-cooked or leftover chicken is also a nice addition, but by no means essential.

Mix all your dressing ingredients together in a bowl and put to the side. Chop all your veg—we normally use a regular knife and slice as thinly as we can, but if you have a mandoline then this would probably do a great job and be much quicker. You can peel the carrots into ribbons, but it is quite nice to have them a bit thicker and crunchier. Mix all your vegetables in your lunch container, adding the shredded chicken if using.

Wrap your herbs separately in a few pieces of slightly damp paper towels. Transfer your dressing to a small jam jar and make sure that it is shut properly.

Come lunchtime
Half an hour before eating, dress your salad and mix well. When you are ready to lunch, sprinkle the herbs over the top before diving in.

TIP FOR BULKING UP

If you are feeling particularly hungry and salad alone won't cut it, add a portion of rice vermicelli noodles. Just place the dried noodles in a large heatproof bowl, add enough boiling water to cover them, and leave for 5 minutes with a clean dish towel over the top to prevent the steam from escaping. Drain and refresh with some cold water—then drain again and add to your lunch container (the noodles should be the bottom layer, with the veg going on top).

TIP FOR SPEEDING UP

If you want to simplify the process, add the herbs on top of the veg and wait until lunch to mix everything together. It would be dishonest of us to claim that we never unceremoniously shove all of our ingredients in a Tupperware and hope for the best.

MEXICAN-STYLE CORN

Preparation time: 15 minutes
Makes 1 serving

- *1 ear of corn*
- *2 tbsp mayonnaise*
- *½ tsp dried chili flakes*
- *2 tbsp finely grated hard cheese (Parmesan*

or pecorino are perfect, although Cheddar also works well)
- *handful of chopped cilantro (optional)*
- *½ lime*

Okay, not technically green, but crunchy and fresh...and covered with cheese. A microwave is handy here to warm the corn, but don't worry if you don't have access to one, as this tastes just as good at room temperature. Cold corn is not good though, so don't refrigerate it.

Bring a medium-sized pan of water to a boil. If your corn has a husk, remove it now then cut the ear in half. Once the water is boiling, add the corn and cook for 3–4 minutes, or until the water begins to boil again.

While the corn is cooking, prepare your other ingredients for transporting to work. Tiny jam jars or plastic containers are perfect for storing the mayonnaise. Chili flakes can be wrapped in parchment paper or newspaper, while the cheese is best stored in a small Tupperware.

Once the corn is cooked, drain and pat dry. Don't wait for it to cool down but wrap immediately in foil.

Come lunchtime
Unwrap your corn and arrange on a plate. If you have a microwave, you could heat it for 1 minute. Spread the corn thinly with mayonnaise and sprinkle over the chili flakes, grated cheese, and cilantro. Generously squeeze lime over the top, and enjoy. Remember to floss your teeth before talking to anyone.

WHOLESOME AND HEALTHY: *Wake your brain with some spice*

MOROCCAN SPINACH

Preparation time: 30 minutes
Makes 2 servings

- 1 tbsp extra-virgin olive oil
- 1 onion, thinly sliced
- 1 tsp cumin seeds
- 1 x 14½ oz can chopped tomatoes
- 1 tsp ras el hanout
- Pinch of sugar
- salt and freshly ground black pepper

- 1 garlic clove
- 1 x 5 oz bag of fresh spinach
- 1 x 15 oz can chickpeas, drained
- juice of 1 lemon
- crusty bread, to serve

This dish was initially inspired by Valentine Warner's divine recipe for Prawns Tangiers which appeared in the UK's The Sunday Times Style many moons ago. The clipping from which it was cooked is now firmly coated in grease—always a good sign.

The night before

Heat the olive oil in a small heavy-bottomed casserole dish. Add the onion to the pan along with the cumin seeds and cook gently for a few minutes.

Stir in the chopped tomatoes. Give the empty can a rinse and then add this splash of tomatoey water to the pan along with the ras el hanout, sugar, and salt and pepper. Crush the garlic into the pan. Add the spinach and stir with a wooden spoon until they have softened. This will take a few minutes. Then add the drained chickpeas and leave to simmer, lid on, for about 20 minutes. Toward the end, add the lemon juice and taste to check the seasoning. Put the lid on and leave overnight.

In the morning

Simply pop into a container. You could also pack some bread separately to enjoy alongside this dish come lunchtime.

If you are making this first thing, allow to cool for 5 minutes before spooning into a Tupperware container.

Come lunchtime

Tastes delicious reheated or at room temperature.

WHOLESOME AND HEALTHY: *Wake your brain with some spice*

CHEAT'S BÁNH MÌ

Preparation time: 15 minutes

Makes 1 baguette

- 1 frozen ready-to-bake baguette
- ½ tbsp rice wine vinegar
- 1 scallion, sliced into long strands
- ½ carrot, peeled into ribbons
- good squirt of mayonnaise
- handful of leftover roast chicken, pork, or beef
- good squirt of Sriracha chili sauce
- 1½ in chunk of cucumber, sliced into 6 circles
- 3 radishes, sliced into circles
- small handful of cilantro, leaves picked and washed
- small handful of mint, leaves picked and washed

Baguettes are indisputably one of the most delicious bread products in the world, but unfortunately they go stale pretty quickly. We like to keep the frozen ready-to-bake variety on hand: simply take them out of the freezer, bake for 10 minutes, et voilà, a lovely crusty baguette. Obviously you can fill them with anything, but they are particularly good for bánh mì, which traditionally call for a crisper baguette.

Preheat your oven to 350°F. While it's heating, chop the veg. Once the oven is hot, add the baguette and cook for 12 minutes (or a couple of minutes longer than the instructions direct—you want to slightly overcook it to avoid any potential sog factor) until crisp and golden brown. Leave to cool.

Add the rice wine vinegar to the scallion and carrot and leave to sit.

Cut the baguette in half lengthwise, leaving a hinge down one side. Rip out a bit of the doughy middle in both halves, so that there's a hollow for the filling. Spread the bottom with mayonnaise, layer with your meat of choice and squirt over the chili sauce. Lay the cucumber slices in a line, repeat with the radish slices, then add the pickled onion and carrot (squeeze out any excess liquid first). Wrap tightly in foil and enclose the cilantro and mint separately in slightly damp paper towel.

Come lunchtime
Add the cilantro and mint to your baguette just before eating.

2: INDULGENT AND DECADENT

Whether you are celebrating or commiserating, sometimes, when it comes to lunch, you feel like treating yourself. Maybe it's the day after payday, and you've bought some groceries after eating only pasta for two weeks and want to make something a bit special, or maybe it's been a difficult week, and you fancy eating something more decadent than usual to buoy your spirits. Whatever the reason: don't fight it. Indulgent doesn't have to equal expensive or "bad for you." The recipes in this chapter are no more difficult or time-consuming than any of the others. They use ingredients that are slightly out of the ordinary (artichoke) or luxurious combinations (chorizo and roasted pepper; falafel and eggplant; halloumi and avocado) that elevate them above your everyday fare. All should leave you with a warm glow inside, a sense of satisfaction, and an improved readiness to face the rest of the day.

GRILLED HALLOUMI, VEGETABLE
& AVOCADO COUSCOUS

Preparation time: a paltry 22 minutes. Makes 1 serving

- *handful of cherry tomatoes*
- *salt*
- *extra-virgin olive oil, for drizzling*
- *1 pepper (red or yellow)*
- *2 oz couscous*
- *handful of green beans*

- *halloumi (at least 4 slices)*
- *handful of arugula (optional)*
- *½ avocado*
- *squeeze of lemon juice*
- *1 smoked herring fillet, flaked (optional)*

O*ne of our absolute favorite lunch dishes. You need to eat it to believe it. It should be made in the morning before you leave for work and takes 22 minutes. We know that halloumi is best eaten straight away, but there is just no better cheese for this dish.*

In the morning

Turn the oven on full blast and put a handful of cherry tomatoes in a small roasting dish. Drizzle the tomatoes with a little salt and olive oil, then place the dish as close as possible to the heat source in your oven. Time is of the essence here.

Heat a griddle pan on the stove until very hot. Put a pan of salted water on to boil— this is for the green beans. Put a freshly replenished kettle on. This is for the couscous and a cup of tea, if you'd like.

Start with the pepper. Chop into roughly pizza-topping-sized slices and cook on the griddle pan until you achieve a char-grilled effect. No need for oil. While these are grilling, empty a portion of couscous into a largish Tupperware container. Cover gently with the boiling water from the kettle and then cover with a dish towel.

Take a quick look at the roasting tomatoes. They will be ready when they have burst a little and the juices are running.

Add the green beans to the pan of boiling water and blanch for a few minutes. You want these to be still crunchy.

Remove the cooked peppers from the griddle and spray the pan with a little cooking oil to stop the cheese sticking. Slice as much halloumi as you like and griddle until you get the chargrilled lines and the cheese is soft and squishy.

The couscous in your Tupperware should be ready now. Run a fork through it to separate the grains and add a drizzle of olive oil to it. Stir in the roasted tomatoes and all their lovely juices. Top with the grilled peppers, halloumi, green beans and a little arugula if you wish.

INDULGENT AND DECADENT: Salads that aren't like salads

Slice an avocado in half and squeeze some lemon juice over it. Place half snugly in the Tupperware and the other half in the fridge wrapped in plastic wrap. Top with the herring flakes, if using.

Come lunchtime
Open your lunchbox and remove the avocado half. Using a spoon, scoop out lovely chunks and add to the dish. Finally, give everything a good stir. Bat the inevitable probing forks away from your plate. Enjoy.

INDULGENT AND DECADENT: *Salads that aren't like salads*

MARINA RIVIERA - AMALFI

FALAFEL WITH YOGURT, EGGPLANT & RED CABBAGE SALAD

Preparation time: 10 minutes, plus 40 minutes cooking
Makes 1 generous serving

- 1 eggplant
- 2 tbsp extra-virgin olive oil
- salt and freshly ground black pepper
- 6 ready-made falafels
- ⅛ red cabbage
- 1¼ in piece of cucumber
- ¼ red onion
- 4–5 cherry tomatoes, halved

- 1 pita or flatbread
- Sriracha chili sauce (optional)

For the yogurt dressing
- 4 tbsp plain yogurt
- juice of ½ lime
- salt and freshly ground black pepper
- 1 tbsp any chopped fresh green herb

The best falafels we have tasted so far are from L'As du Fallafel on Rue des Rosiers in Paris. This recipe is an homage to them. This dish is all in the careful packing and the assembly at work. You can make everything the night before, but be sure to keep the dressing in the fridge.

The night before

Preheat the oven to 375°F. Chop your eggplant up into 1¼ in chunks and lay on a roasting tray. Drizzle over the olive oil and the salt and pepper, and roast for 35 minutes or until golden and squishy. Ten minutes before the end of the cooking time, add the falafels to the oven dish. When the time is up, leave to cool on the counter under some aluminum foil.

In the morning

Grate the cabbage into ribbons, the finer the better. Cut or grate the cucumber into small pieces. Finely chop the onion. Add to your designated container along with the cherry tomatoes, cooled falafel, and eggplant.

To prepare the dressing, simply mix all of the ingredients together in a small jam jar or Tupperware. Lightly toast your pita or flatbread and pack separately, in foil or a brown paper bag. Keeping this dish at room temperature for a few hours until lunchtime is fine.

Come lunchtime

Open the pita, or lay out the flatbread. Give your ingredients a good stir before spooning over your pita or flatbread. Drizzle over the yogurt dressing along with some chili sauce, if you keep any at the office.

INDULGENT AND DECADENT: Salads that aren't like salads

POTATO, SMOKED HERRING & MUSTARD SALAD

*Preparation time: roughly 15 minutes potato cooking time,
then 5 minutes to put it all together. Makes 1 serving*

- *4 small potatoes, halved or quartered,
depending on size*
- *1 tbsp crème fraîche*
- *½ tsp whole-grain mustard*
- *½ tsp Dijon mustard*
- *good squeeze of lemon juice*

- *salt and freshly ground black pepper*
- *1 smoked herring fillet, flaked into
large pieces*
- *handful of lettuce leaves—arugula and
spinach also work well*

**The crème fraîche makes this feel quite decadent: balance it out by eating with
some peppery leaves.**

Put water, a pinch of salt, and the potatoes in a medium-sized pan and bring to a boil. Cook until you can stick the end of a knife through the potatoes, around 15 minutes. Drain and run under cold water for a minute, then leave to cool.

Add the crème fraîche and mustards to your tiffin tin or lunch container and mix together, adding lemon juice to thin it out. Once the potatoes are cool, add them and mix so that they're evenly coated. Season generously with salt and pepper and mix again, then add the herring pieces, and fold together gently. Put the leaves in a separate container and keep the herring and potatoes refrigerated while at work.

Come lunchtime
Remove from the fridge about 15 minutes before lunchtime. Serve on a plate for a truly decadent lunch.

If this isn't quite indulgent enough, then why not add a soft-boiled egg? Just add your egg to the boiling potatoes after they have been cooking for 8 minutes. Cook the egg for the remaining 7 minutes, then run under the cold tap after draining the potatoes. Nestle in your salad container, and peel and cut in half at lunchtime to crown your salad.

INDULGENT AND DECADENT: *Salads that aren't like salads*

SPICY SPINACH & FETA PASTRY

Preparation time: 30 minutes
Makes 2 servings

- *4 sheets ready-to-bake filo pastry*
- *½ stick butter*
- *8 oz spinach*
- *½ tsp ground cumin*
- *pinch of dried chili flakes*

- *salt and freshly ground black pepper*
- *1½ in piece of red or green chili, seeded and finely chopped*
- *1 tbsp crumbled feta*

Yes, you do have to brush each layer of filo pastry with butter (or oil if you really must) but the end result is worth it.

Preheat the oven to 400°F. Quickly remove 4 sheets of filo from the packet, laying out on a large, clean cutting board, and covering with a dish towel. Return the rest to the fridge.

Add a spoonful of the butter to a large frying pan and as it begins to melt add the spinach, cumin, chili flakes, and salt and pepper. Put a lid on so that it steams, and leave for 5 minutes. Meanwhile, melt the rest of the butter in a small pan, then take off the heat.

Check the spinach: it should be completely cooked. Add the fresh chili and mix in. Remove from the heat, and push the spinach to one side of the pan with a wooden spoon, squeezing the excess liquid out of it, and pouring it away. Do this a few times, so you get rid of as much liquid as possible.

Working quickly, take the first pastry sheet and use a pastry brush to brush

the surface with melted butter. Lay the second sheet over the top and repeat until you end up with the fourth layer (don't butter this!). Lay the spinach in an even, straight line, lengthwise, about a third of the way from the bottom of the pastry, making sure it goes all the way to the end. Sprinkle the feta over evenly. Fold the bottom piece of pastry (below the spinach) over the top of it. Brush this with butter, and then fold over, forward. Continue turning, brushing the pastry with butter where necessary so that it sticks. You should end up with something that looks like a large sausage roll. Place on a lined baking tray and bake for 15 minutes, turning halfway.

TRANSPORTING TIPS
Your pastry will be quite long, so unless you're very hungry, it should be enough for two. We recommend cutting it in half once it's cooled slightly, and then wrapping it in foil once it's completely cool (otherwise the pastry will become soggy).

INDULGENT AND DECADENT: *Salads that aren't like salads*

PARMA HAM, TOMATO, MOZZARELLA & PESTO SANDWICH

Preparation time: 15 minutes
Makes 1 sandwich

- *½ large ciabatta/1 small ciabatta roll—look out for ones that are suitable for freezing (freeze immediately and use within a month)*
- *1 very generous tbsp pesto*
- *3 slices Parma ham*

- *½ ball of mozzarella, sliced*
- *½ tomato, thickly sliced*
- *pinch of salt*
- *splash of extra-virgin olive oil*
- *handful of basil leaves*

This classic Italian sandwich is so good that you could easily eat two of them— as a friend of ours once did, secretly scarfing our sandwich. Over it? Not really.

If you are using a frozen ciabatta, preheat your oven to 350°F. Bake for 10 minutes and leave to cool.

If you've used a large ciabatta, cut in half, then cut it in half lengthwise, leaving a hinge on one side. Spread the bottom with pesto, then cover with Parma ham, mozzarella, and tomatoes.

Sprinkle salt over the tomatoes, and a splash of oil. Top with basil leaves and close. Wrap firmly in foil or parchment paper secured with string.

Come lunchtime
Unwrap and eat as quickly as possible before someone tries to steal it from you.

SIMPLE GUACAMOLE
& TOMATO SALSA ON RYE

Preparation time: 4 minutes, plus 3 minutes assembly
Makes 1 serving

For the tomato salsa
- 1 garlic clove
- 1 handful of diced tomatoes
- 1 scallion or ½ small red onion
- few basil leaves
- extra-virgin olive oil
- a squeeze of juice from 1 lime, sliced in half
- salt and freshly ground black pepper

For the guacamole
- 1 ripe avocado
- handful of fresh cilantro
- ½ red chili, seeded
- leftover lime juice from salsa
- salt

- 2–3 slices rye bread

This lunch manages to be beautifully light yet indulgent at the same time. Really any bread you have will do (frankly that half empty packet of Ritz crackers would also do the trick), but we think rye works nicely here—two or three slices, depending on the size of your loaf.

In the morning

To make the salsa, finely chop the garlic, along with the tomatoes, scallions, and basil. Place in a small container. Drizzle over a little olive oil and a squeeze of lime juice. Taste and season with plenty of salt and pepper.

To make the guacamole, use a sharp knife to slice the avocado in half. Remove the stone and, using a spoon, scoop out the lovely flesh and add to another container. Finely chop the cilantro and chili and stir into the avocado. Squeeze over the reserved lime juice (this will keep the avocado looking fresh until lunchtime). Sprinkle over some salt little by little, mixing and tasting as you go to get it just right.

Pack your bread in foil or a brown paper bag. Upon arrival at work, the salsa and guacamole could be kept in the fridge if desired.

Come lunchtime

Lay out the slices of rye bread. Spread the salsa mixture on one, and the guacamole on the other two. Take a picture. Feast.

BALT SOURDOUGH SANDWICH

Preparation time: 10 minutes, plus 10 minutes for the bacon to cool, 5 minutes to pack and 10 seconds after the first bite to close your eyes happily and realize that it was worth the effort. Makes 1 sandwich

- *2 slices of sourdough, or another firm bread—this is a sandwich that needs supporting*
- *2 slices bacon*

- *3 slices tomato*
- *3 baby romaine lettuce leaves*
- *½ ripe avocado, sliced*
- *healthy dollop of mayonnaise*

The ultimate pick-me-up, this is the sandwich that inspired us to start thinking more seriously about our lunches. A few key things: make sure your avocado is ripe and try and buy some really nice bread, as this will elevate it from simply a good sandwich to something your colleagues talk about in reverential whispers. Also, it's just as easy to make a couple of these (and it solves the problem of what to do with that spare half an avocado), so why not treat your roommate/boyfriend/girlfriend/ desk buddy and make them one too? This sandwich will make you friends.

In the morning

Heat up a griddle pan until it is really hot and place your bread on it, allowing it to slightly toast for a minute on each side. Remove, put to the side and add the bacon. You shouldn't need any extra fat, but if it starts to stick, add a glob of oil. Cook until super crispy (or to your own personal taste). Once cooked, immediately place on one of the slices of bread. The bacon fat will sink into the bread and make it extra delicious. Leave for 5 minutes while you run around, getting ready for work.

Once the bacon has cooled a bit add the slices of tomato, then the lettuce, then the avocado. Spread the other slice of bread with mayonnaise and place on top. Wrap in either foil or parchment paper and leave uncut until lunch.

PURE DECADENCE

If you have a small thermos you might consider doing something outrageously decadent here, guaranteed to cause a scandal in the workplace. In the morning, heat up a jar of shop-bought hollandaise and transfer to a small thermos. When you're about to eat, simply pour the hollandaise over your asparagus and smile. Ignore the gasps around you.

ASPARAGUS WITH A BOILED EGG IN ITS SHELL

Preparation time: 12 minutes
Makes 1 serving

- 1 or 2 eggs, depending on your appetite
- large bunch of asparagus
- extra-virgin olive oil
- salt and freshly ground black pepper
- Parmesan shavings

For the dressing
- 2 tsp extra-virgin olive oil
- juice of ½ lemon
- pinch of salt

*I*n France, asparagus season is something of an event. Villages devote entire fêtes to it (seriously). And in homes, steamed asparagus is piled high on dish towels in the middle of dining tables; grasping hands reach for those beautiful green-white stems and then dunk them vigorously into their own bowls of mustardy dressing. Yes, asparagus is the main event, not some trivial veg accompaniment as is often the case here. This recipe is no different, with the protein element demoted to the position of garnish.

In the morning

Put a pan of water on to boil. Put a griddle pan on a high heat. Pop an egg or two in the pan of boiling water and cook for 7 minutes. Wash and dry the asparagus, and cut off their woody ends. Put them on a plate and drizzle over some olive oil and salt and pepper. Now, add to the griddle pan and leave to cook for about 10 minutes, turning over halfway. You want those trendy black char marks.

When the eggs are ready, remove from the water and run under the cold tap to halt the cooking. Prepare a Tupperware container long enough to fit your asparagus in. Once the asparagus is ready (broadly speaking, when floppy), place directly in the container. Using a vegetable peeler, shave some Parmesan flakes over the hot asparagus. Be generous with yourself here—no use crying over insufficient Parmesan at work.

Nestle the eggs in with the asparagus and prepare the dressing in a little container. By the time you get to work the dish will have cooled so you could keep it in the fridge, but remember to take it out at 11:30 a.m. as it should be enjoyed at room temperature.

Come lunchtime
Lay your asparagus out nicely on a plate. Peel your eggs, slice in half and arrange on your plate. Drizzle over the dressing.

INDULGENT AND DECADENT: *Being indulgent with vegetables*

ARTICHOKE WITH
A MUSTARD DRESSING

Preparation time: 5 minutes, plus 45 minutes cooking
Makes 1 serving

- 1 artichoke
- 4 whole garlic cloves
- 1 lemon, sliced in half
- 1 bay leaf
- salt

For the dressing
- ¾ cup extra-virgin olive oil
- 1½ tbsp Dijon mustard
- salt and freshly ground black pepper
- 1 tbsp red wine vinegar

One rainy summer day, we decided to bring a cooked artichoke to work for lunch and it caused unprecedented havoc. A colleague exclaimed that she had never ever seen it eaten in this manner, another was surprised to see it as a centerpiece instead of a mere pizza topping—so we've explained how to eat and prepare it here in some detail.

Artichokes are a rare treat, a lunch to be enjoyed and cherished. By nature, impossible to eat quickly, their extravagance lies in the haughty length of time it takes to eat them (we're talking 12 minutes here). They are a tease amongst vegetables, tasting sweeter and subtler the more undressed and the closer you get to the heart.

Note: The dressing quantities here may seem large, but far worse than having too much is running out. And anyway, it'll keep for use in something the next day if you don't finish it.

The night before

Take the artichoke and pull off any tough or sad-looking lower petals toward the bottom. Next, trim the stem, resisting the temptation to hack too much off as, frankly, it's the second best bit (after the heart).

Place the artichoke in a large pan and cover with plenty of water. Add the garlic cloves, lemon, bay leaf, and salt. Pop on a lid and bring the water to a boil. Turn the heat down to prevent water splashing and spitting all over the shop, and leave to simmer for about 45 minutes, or until the stem is soft and the petals can be easily picked. Add all the dressing ingredients to a wide-rimmed jar. Using tongs, fish out the artichoke, and perhaps with a bit of help from a dish towel to prevent scalding, lower it upside down into a mug, stem facing the ceiling and leave to drain overnight. On the countertop is fine.

In the morning
Pack the artichoke in foil and don't forget the dressing.

Come lunchtime
Give the jar a good shake and pop on a plate with the artichoke. To eat, pick a petal from the artichoke and, holding

the tip (i.e., the bit that you gripped to pull it off), dip the other end in the dressing. Using your bottom teeth, scrape the "meat" off and eat, discarding the rest of the petal. You can eat the petals whole when you have almost reached the heart . . . they almost melt in the mouth.

Once you've eaten all of the petals you'll need to peel the revealed furry bit off (the choke) before eating the heart and the stem.

SPANISH LUNCH:
CHORIZO, EGG & POTATO SALAD

Preparation time: 20 minutes
Makes 1 serving

- *8–10 small or new potatoes*
- *2 eggs, at room temperature*
- *6 in piece of chorizo sausage*
- *extra-virgin olive oil for drizzling*
- *1 tbsp freshly chopped chives*
- *salt*

This recipe was inspired by our cheap and cheerful Spanish holidays. A buttery tasting yellow potato works well here. But really any small salad variety will do. This dish is best prepared in the morning before work.

Wash the potatoes and if on the large side, chop in half, adding to a pan of cold, salted water as you go. Bring to a boil, and simmer until they are cooked and can be pierced easily with a knife, usually about 10–15 minutes.

To save time and washing up, cook your eggs in the same pan as the potatoes. Cook for about 7 minutes for a soft-yolked egg before removing from the pan and running under the cold tap.

Meanwhile, chop the chorizo up into small chunks and heat a nonstick pan on the stove. Simply add the chopped chorizo—resisting the temptation to use olive oil—and cook until the fat begins to run and the sausage is crispy in places. Drain the cooked potatoes in a colander and add to your lunch pail. Top with the cooked chorizo, a drizzle of olive oil, and the chives. Give it a stir and sprinkle over some salt.

Wrap the 2 eggs in their shells separately in paper towels. On arrival at work, this dish is best left at room temperature.

Come lunchtime
Peel your boiled eggs and cut into segments, topping your decadent potato dish.

INDULGENT AND DECADENT: Star ingredient – chorizo

CHORIZO WITH COUSCOUS, ROASTED PEPPERS & TOMATOES

Preparation time: 12 minutes. Makes 1 serving

- 6 in piece of chorizo sausage
- 1 yellow or red pepper
- 5–6 cherry tomatoes, halved
- 2 oz couscous
- spinach leaves or salad leaves

If you're making this in the morning, you could fry some extra chorizo to have on a poached egg for breakfast.

Put the kettle on, and place a large frying pan on a medium heat. Chop the chorizo into ½ in chunks before adding to the dry pan. The fat from the sausage should soon start to run, creating a perfect frying environment for the pepper and tomatoes.

While the chorizo is beginning to cook, remove the seeds and white flesh from the pepper before slicing it into strips. Once the fat has run and the pan is full of red juices, add the pepper and the cherry tomatoes.

Turn your attention to the couscous. Add a portion to your lunch receptacle, and pour over boiling water, immersing the couscous with a little water over the top. Cover with a dish towel and leave to plump for a few minutes before separating with a fork.

Once the chorizo is getting crispy and the tomatoes and peppers have taken on some color, turn the heat off and pour over the couscous, taking care to include all the juices. Top with some spinach leaves, or any other green leaf, and transport to work. We keep this one at room temperature.

INDULGENT AND DECADENT: *Star ingredient – chorizo*

CHORIZO & LIMA BEAN STEW-ETTE WITH CRUSTY BREAD ROLL

Preparation time: 10 minutes, plus 10 minutes simmering. Makes 2 servings

- 8 in piece of chorizo sausage
- 1 onion, finely chopped
- handful of green cabbage leaves
- ½ tsp dried thyme
- 1 tsp smoked paprika
- 1 x 15 oz can lima beans
- 1 x 14½ oz can chopped tomatoes
- crusty bread roll, to serve

A very simple dish involving mostly common pantry ingredients. If you don't like cabbage, it's just as good without.

In the morning

Put a pan on a medium to low heat. Chop up the chorizo sausage into chunks and dry-fry. Finely chop the onion, and if the fat from the chorizo has started to run, add to the pan. Leave to soften for a few minutes while you get on with the cabbage. Slice and chop finely, discarding any tough bits. Add to the pan along with the thyme and paprika and mix well, coating with all the lovely red juice from the chorizo.

Drain the can of lima beans and add along with the chopped tomatoes. Stir and then leave to simmer for 10 minutes.

Once cooled, transfer into your container and begin your commute.

Come lunchtime

This can be enjoyed at room temperature or reheated. Eat with a bit of crusty bread.

INDULGENT AND DECADENT: *Star ingredient – chorizo*

DECONSTRUCTED PESTO PASTA

Preparation time: 15 minutes
Makes 1 serving

- *1½ tbsp pine nuts*
- *4 tsp extra-virgin olive oil*
- *1 garlic clove, thinly sliced*
- *1 tsp chili flakes*
- *1 portion of dried pasta (farfalle is nice here)*

- *salt and freshly ground black pepper*
- *Parmesan shavings*
- *large handful of fresh basil*
- *handful of cherry tomatoes (optional)*

Homemade pesto is such a treat. It keeps well in jars in the fridge for several days, and is easily whipped into action for your packed lunch. The pasta can, of course, also be cooked the night before and stored in your Tupperware container to retain its moisture. But as it is so quick to cook, more often than not we make it in the morning. Here is one of our favorite pesto pasta recipes, plus a few variations.

Bring a large pan of salted water to a boil. Put a small pan on the heat and dry-fry the pine nuts until golden. Add them into a container, then add 2 teaspoons of olive oil to the pan they came from and pop back on the heat. Add the sliced garlic to the oil along with the chili flakes. Keep a close eye on the garlic. You don't want it crispy, you just want to soften it a little before adding it to the container.

Once your pan of water is boiling, add the pasta and cook according to the instructions on the box. Drain and stir into the chili and garlic nut mix, coating evenly. Add an extra drizzle of olive oil, and season well with salt and pepper. Shave over some Parmesan (be generous with yourself here) and top with a large handful of basil leaves. Pop in the fridge once the pasta has cooled if you're cooking the night before.

Come lunchtime
Toss the pasta, ensuring an even spread of basil. Halve the cherry tomatoes, if using, and enjoy.

TRADITIONAL PESTO

- 2 tbsp pine nuts
- large handful of fresh basil
- 1 garlic clove, crushed
- 2 tbsp extra-virgin olive oil
- 2 tbsp grated Parmesan

Put a small pan on a medium heat and dry fry the pine nuts until toasted. Put in a flat-bottomed mixing bowl or a large liquid measuring cup along with the remaining ingredients and blitz with a hand blender until smooth.

TOMATO & ALMOND PESTO

- 2 tbsp whole unskinned almonds
- 4 tbsp grated Parmesan
- handful of cherry tomatoes
- pinch of sea salt
- 2 tbsp fresh basil
- 1 garlic clove, grated
- 1 tbsp extra-virgin olive oil

Put a small pan on a medium heat and dry-fry the almonds until lightly toasted. Put in a flat-bottomed mixing bowl or a large liquid measuring cup along with the remaining ingredients and blitz with a hand blender until smooth.

ENGLISH PESTO

- 2 tbsp pine nuts
- 4 tbsp finely grated Berkswell cheese—if you can't get a hold of this, Parmesan will do the trick
- 2 handfuls of fresh parsley
- 1 tbsp extra-virgin olive oil

Put a small pan on a medium heat and dry-fry the pine nuts until toasted and golden. Put in a flat-bottomed mixing bowl or a large liquid measuring cup along with the remaining ingredients and blitz until smooth.

SANDWICH
BOX

3: WHEN YOU ARE CHAINED TO YOUR DESK

*I*t's 12:58 p.m. Suddenly the office is deserted: you can almost see the tumbleweed as your colleagues amble off to grab the remaining bench in the sunshine, or fight it out over the last cafeteria baked potato. You, however, are buried, working to an impossibly tight deadline. Pal, you are going NOWHERE. Lucky then that you are a person of exceptional foresight and knew that it was going to be one of those days. You have with you a packed lunch to be enjoyed al desko. So far, so smart. Except . . . eating at your workstation has its own complicated set of unwritten rules. Here is our guide to the etiquette of eating at your desk.

• Reheated leftover curry or chili con carne is unacceptable. People more senior than you will walk past and say things like, "*What is that smell?*" which is embarrassing and compromises your public enjoyment of a perfectly good (if fragrant) meal.

• Avoid anything loud and crunchy that requires lots of chewing. A crusty roll filled with bacon is no good. You can guarantee that the second you've taken a bite, your boss will come over and try and ask you something. You will nod while frantically chewing, swallow too quickly to compensate, and choke. Best avoided.

• Greasy foodstuffs will come back to haunt you in the form of translucent grease stains on important documents, or nasty stuff on your mouse. Don't risk it.

That's not to say you shouldn't have a nice lunch. You are slaving away after all: you need something to look forward to. But choose something easy to eat while working—a soothing soup, poured piping hot from a thermos that you can sip from a mug, or a simple pasta that you can eat with a fork in one hand. Or, if it's a day when you would really like to be in the park, basking in the sun, bring the outside in and have a desk picnic with an open-faced sandwich or a DIY antipasti plate.

We could extol the virtues of the thermos for hours: an impossibly clever invention, perfect for al fresco tea, coffee, and, of course, al desko soup.

The soups that follow can be made in the morning if you have time or cooked the night before and reheated first thing prior to the thermos transfer. You'll feel particularly pleased with yourself if you remember to pack a piece of crusty bread, wrapped in parchment paper. Dunk into the soup with abandon, but hide the crumbs.

It's almost impossible to make just one portion of soup. These recipes serve three on average. If you don't want to eat the same lunch two days in a row, freeze the extra batches in medium-sized sandwich bags. The night before, remove one from the freezer and place in a bowl (still in its bag) to begin defrosting. In the morning, slip the contents out of the bag and into a pan on the lowest heat on the stove. Now would be your optimum shower and readying time. When the mixture is bubbling—after about 25 minutes—it's ready for your thermos.

BLACK BEAN SOUP

Preparation time: 30 minutes
Makes 2 servings

- 1 x 15 oz can black beans
- 2 tbsp extra-virgin olive oil
- 1 large red onion, chopped
- ½ tsp ground cumin
- pinch of dried chili flakes
- 1 garlic clove, sliced

- 1 bay leaf
- handful of freshly chopped cilantro
- salt and freshly ground black pepper
- 1 cup chicken stock
- squeeze of lime juice

This hearty yet surprisingly low-fat soup is perfect for the sort of gray autumn day that feels like winter, when you wouldn't want to pop outside to buy lunch even if you had the time. If you want to bulk it up a bit you could add some fried bacon bits or crumbled chorizo at the same time as the extra beans.

Empty the can of beans into a bowl, without draining away the liquid. Remove a little less than half a mugful of the beans from the bowl, and keep to one side.

Add the oil to a large pan (you will blend everything in this later), and cook the onion on a medium heat until it begins to turn soft and translucent. Add the cumin and chili flakes and leave for 1 minute, then add the garlic and cook for a further 2 minutes. Add the beans and their juice, the bay leaf, cilantro, salt and pepper, and chicken stock, and bring to a simmer.

Remove from the heat and fish out the bay leaf (set aside). Using a hand blender, blend all the ingredients. Add the beans that you set aside earlier, then bring everything back to a simmer and add the bay leaf back. Taste and adjust the seasoning and add a splash of water if the consistency is too thick.

Come lunchtime
Pour from your thermos and add a squeeze of fresh lime juice.

SPICY ROOT VEG SOUP

*Preparation time: 15 minutes, plus 35 minutes cooking
(while you're getting ready), 5 minutes blending
Makes 3 servings*

- *1–2 tbsp butter*
- *2 tsp extra-virgin olive oil*
- *1 onion, roughly chopped*
- *1 lb root veg (carrot, parsnip, turnip, etc.)*
- *1 tsp garam masala*
- *1 tsp salt*
- *freshly ground black pepper*
- *1 fresh chili, seeded and chopped*

This is a soup we make all winter. Really any root vegetable combination you have will do: experiment!

Put the butter and olive oil in a large heavy-bottomed pan and place on a low heat. Add the onion to the pan, stirring well. Fill a small pot or saucepan with 6 cups of water and put it on to boil.

Peel the root vegetables and chop into cubes, keeping an eye on the softening onions as you go. Add the garam masala to the onion, stirring well, and leave for a minute or two before turning the heat up to medium and adding the vegetable chunks and the salt and pepper. Mix well to coat evenly, then put the lid on and leave to steam for 2 minutes while

you chop the chili. Add the chili to the pan, followed by the 6 cups of hot water, and leave to simmer, lid off, for 30 minutes. Turn the heat off and leave to rest for a few minutes before blending to a smooth soup with your hand blender—probably best to wear an apron if you're doing this in the morning. Using a ladle, and ideally a funnel, pour into your thermos. Close firmly.

Come lunchtime
Locate your preferred coffee mug (we've all got a favorite), and pour in the soup.

WHEN YOU ARE CHAINED TO YOUR DESK: *Soups and a note on the thermos*

CARROT & LENTIL SOUP

Preparation time: 15 minutes, plus 30 minutes cooking
Makes 3–4 servings

- 1 tbsp extra-virgin olive oil
- 1 onion, finely chopped
- 1 garlic clove, crushed
- 1 fresh red chili, seeded and finely chopped
- 4 carrots, roughly chopped
- 1 red pepper, seeded and chopped

- 2 oz red lentils
- ½ tsp ground coriander
- ½ tsp ground turmeric
- ½ tsp paprika
- ½ tsp ground cumin
- 1 tsp salt

A hearty and economical soup, given that carrots are one of the cheapest vegetables around. We like this soup very thick, so do feel free to augment the water quantity according to your preference.

Fill a small pot or saucepan with 4 cups of water and put on to boil. Heat the olive oil in a large pan on a medium to low heat and add the onion, garlic, and chili, stirring well and leaving to soften for a minute or two.

Add the carrots and pepper to the pan, stirring well. Cook for a further 2 minutes before adding the lentils and spices. Stir for a minute before adding the 4 cups of water and the salt. Bring it all to a boil then turn down to a simmer for 20 minutes—or until the carrots are tender. Purée using a hand blender and transfer a portion to a thermos. The remaining soup can be left on the stove, lid on, until you get back from work.

SPINACH, TOMATO & FETA PASTA SALAD

Preparation time: 5 minutes, plus 25 minutes cooking
Makes 2 servings

- 1 tbsp extra-virgin olive oil
- 3 anchovies
- 1 garlic clove, crushed
- 1 x 14½ oz can tomatoes
- 1 tbsp capers
- 2 portions of fusilli pasta
- handful of fresh baby spinach leaves
- 2 tbsp crumbled feta cheese

A friend (Dave, who happens to be chairman of the North London Paella Appreciation Society) once admitted that he liked lunches that could be eaten with one hand, leaving the other free to hold something, like a book. This recipe is ideal for those, like Dave, who enjoy combining the lunch hour with a little multitasking.

The night before
Make your tomato sauce: in a small pan, gently heat the olive oil and the anchovies. Once the anchovies have dissolved into a paste, add the crushed garlic to the pan. Cook the garlic for a minute before adding the can of tomatoes and the capers. Leave to reduce, on the lowest heat, for at least 20 minutes.

While the sauce is cooking, put a pan of salted water on a high heat. Once boiling, add the pasta and cook until just al dente. Drain and stir the pasta into the tomato sauce before adding a portion to a lunch container. Leave to cool on the side before popping in the fridge overnight.

In the morning
Open the container and top the pasta with two handfuls of fresh spinach leaves along with the feta cheese. Transport to work.

Come lunchtime
Enjoy at room temperature or slightly reheated.

WHEN YOU ARE CHAINED TO YOUR DESK: All you neeed is a fork

EGGPLANT CAVIAR

Preparation time: 10 minutes, plus 40 minutes cooking
Makes 2 servings

- 2 eggplants
- 1 garlic clove
- 2 tsp extra-virgin olive oil
- salt and freshly ground black pepper

- ½ tsp ground cumin
- 2 tsp lemon juice

- crusty bread

This is a delicious light lunch. Adjust the seasoning according to your taste, and feel free to replace the bread with raw crudités if you're cutting down on gluten.

Preheat the oven to 350°F. Poke the eggplants with a fork to prevent any messy explosions (we speak from experience) and pop directly in the oven. Leave to cook for 40 minutes.

Speedy tip: if you have a microwave, poke the eggplants and pop them in for 15 minutes.

When the eggplants have softened, remove from the oven and leave to cool for a minute or two in a colander. Slice in half, then scoop out the flesh with a spoon and add to a bowl (you could also include some of the skin if you wish, for texture). Add the remaining ingredients, and, using a hand blender, blend to a smooth paste.

Taste and adjust the seasoning before spooning into a container.

Come lunchtime
Enjoy this on a few slices of crusty bread or baguette.

From top to bottom: spicy chickpea dip, rosemary and lima bean smash, eggplant caviar

SPICY CHICKPEA DIP

Preparation time: 10 minutes
Makes 1 serving

- 3 tsp nut oil, such as hazelnut or sesame (or use extra-virgin olive oil)
- ½ onion, very thinly sliced
- 1 x 15 oz can chickpeas
- 2 garlic cloves
- ½ tsp ground cumin
- ½ tsp cayenne pepper
- ½ tsp ground coriander
- squeeze of lemon or lime juice
- salt
- handful of cherry tomatoes
- 2 slices rye bread

A kind of chunky hummus. This is a recipe we come back to again and again.

Put a small frying pan on a medium heat and add 1 teaspoon of the oil. Add the onion and leave to soften while you prepare the rest of the dip.

Empty the can of chickpeas into a colander and drain the liquid. Transfer the chickpeas to a bowl, and pour over the remaining nut oil. Using a hand blender, blend the chickpeas to a paste. Don't worry if there are lumps. Crush the garlic (or grate using a microplane grater if you have one) over the chickpea dip. Add the spices, along with the lemon juice, and mix well. Add a pinch or two of salt, then taste to check the seasoning and add more if needed.

The onions should be nicely cooked now, take them off the heat and simply stir into the chickpea dip. Transfer to a container. Pop the tomatoes into a paper bag, along with the slices of rye bread, or whatever you have to hand.

Come lunchtime
Spread the dip over the slices of bread, and top with the cherry tomatoes, sliced in half. Sprinkle some salt over and enjoy.

ROSEMARY & LIMA BEAN SMASH

Preparation time: 3 minutes
Makes 1 serving

- *1 tbsp extra-virgin olive oil*
- *1 garlic clove, finely chopped*
- *1 tsp chili flakes*
- *sprig of rosemary*
- *1 x 15 oz can lima beans*

- *1 heaped tbsp crème fraîche*
- *1 tsp Maldon sea salt*
- *2 slices bread*
- *handful of cherry tomatoes*

This doesn't keep for as long as the eggplant caviar or the spicy chickpea dip, so we would advise only making one batch at a time

In the morning

Heat the olive oil in a small pan on the lowest setting and add the garlic, along with the chili flakes. Leave the garlic to soften but make sure it doesn't get crispy—no more than a minute. Peel the leaves off your rosemary and chop as finely as you can before adding to the pan for a minute to infuse in the oil. Remove from the heat and pour the olive oil mixture into a tall bowl.

Drain the beans, and add to the bowl along with the crème fraîche and sea salt. Using a hand blender, blitz until smooth. Check the seasoning and consistency, adding more salt and crème fraîche if necessary. Pop in a container. Pack the bread and tomatoes separately.

Come lunchtime

Spread the smash on your bread. Chop the tomatoes in half and lay facing up on your spread. Sprinkle over some salt. Enjoy.

WHEN YOU ARE CHAINED TO YOUR DESK: *Desktop dipping*

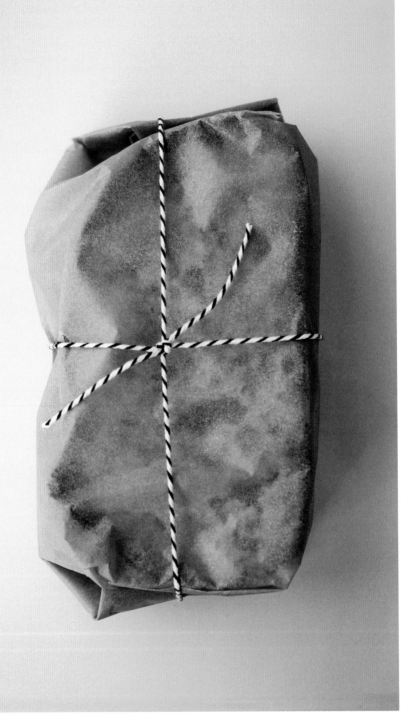

THE SANDWICH HALL OF FAME

....

Sometimes only a sandwich will do. You can pick up all of these and eat them while still typing. Some barely count as recipes, but it's easy to forget the delicious simplicity of the classic two-ingredient sandwich. This Hall of Fame serves as a kitchen prompt.

....

HOW TO PACK YOUR SANDWICH

You can get plastic sandwich cases now, but we always worry that these might not be quite large enough to house our sometimes hefty creations. Plus, there is something really enjoyable about the act of unwrapping your sandwich.

Foil

Classic and reliable but always feels a bit wasteful. Try not to use too much, fold it tightly and make sure it doesn't come into contact with any sharp objects (e.g., keys) in your bag.

Parchment paper

Our preferred sandwich wrapping. As with foil, try not to use too much, fold it tightly and secure with a piece of string.

Plastic wrap

Unpleasant and makes for a sweaty sandwich. Avoid.

AVOIDING THE SOG

There are few things as disappointing in life as a soggy sandwich. Sometimes the worst will happen, but you can act to avoid this:

• A thin layer of butter on bread acts as a sealant.

• Blot your tomato slices, especially if very ripe, on a piece of paper towel to absorb, before adding to your sandwich.

• Always wash lettuce, but dry it properly before adding to your sandwich.

• Don't be stingy with condiments, but be aware that they will absorb into the bread and soften it.

And finally—if you are really struggling to keep your sandwiches from going soggy, simply pack the fillings suggested hereafter in a container, put two slices of bread in a brown bag, and assemble the thing at work. There is no shame in admitting defeat.

CLASSIC CHEESE & TOMATO

Preparation time: 5 minutes
Makes 1 sandwich

- *2 slices multigrain or seeded bread*
- *enough butter to thinly spread on one slice*
- *enough cheese (we like a sharp Cheddar or a nutty Jarlsberg) to cover 1 slice*
- *½ large ripe tomato or 5 cherry*
- *tomatoes, sliced*
- *enough mayonnaise to generously spread on 1 slice*
- *freshly ground black pepper*

Like bread and butter, the combination of cheese and tomato seems so obvious, so natural, that it's easy to think it doesn't merit a recipe. Unfortunately, lackluster cheese and tomato sandwiches do still exist. The key is freshly ground black pepper. Follow the method below and never be disappointed again.

Lightly toast your bread and leave to cool. This sandwich has a high sog risk factor, so it's important to do all you can to prevent it. Toasting the bread helps, and also makes it pleasantly crisp. Once cool, spread one slice thinly with butter, and cover with cheese. Blot the sliced tomato with a paper towel to soak up any excess sog-inducing moisture, and lay the slices on top of the cheese. Spread the other slice of bread with mayo—be generous but don't go wild. Grind a good amount of black pepper over the tomatoes, then sandwich together and wrap securely in parchment paper. Slice just before you eat.

TUNA WITH BASIL & CAPERS

....

Preparation time: 5 minutes
Makes 1 sandwich

- 1 x 5 oz can tuna
- 2 tbsp capers
- freshly ground black pepper
- 1 tbsp mayonnaise

- handful of basil leaves, if you have them
- 2 slices bread (also works well in a pita—
see page 127)

....

*I*t may be sacrilegious to suggest adding anything but the traditional ingredients to tuna (we've seen lengthy comment threads on a company intranet on this topic—seriously), but try this once and you will (probably) become a caper convert.

....

Drain the can of tuna (in either water or oil, although water is healthier) and add to a bowl. Roughly chop the capers—you don't want them to be very fine, but neither do you want large whole capers. Tuna and capers are salty enough, so simply grind over some black pepper, and stir in the mayonnaise. Add a handful of ripped basil leaves, and taste the filling, adding more pepper if necessary. Assemble your sandwich.

SAUCISSON & CORNICHON

Preparation time: 3 minutes
Makes 1 sandwich

- 2 slices multigrain bread
- soft butter

- 2 in piece of saucisson (dried salami)
- 1 tbsp cornichons or gherkins

A classic combination. The annoying thing about dried salami is that it is impossible to tell in the shop whether or not it's a good one: you'll only know once you've tasted it. This recipe calls for the gamblers amongst you to take a chance on this cured French sausage (available from most deli counters in supermarkets).

B utter both sides of the bread. Using a sharp knife, slice the saucisson as thinly as you can. Peel the "skin" off the rounds. Layer the saucisson on one side of the sandwich.

Slice the cornichons in half and pop on top of the saucisson. Cover with the other slice of bread, then slice the sandwich in half. Wrap in foil.

SMOKED SALMON & CELERIAC REMOULADE

*Preparation time: 7 minutes for the celeriac, 5 minutes to pack everything up,
2 minutes to assemble, 1.5 minutes to devour. Makes 1 sandwich*

- ⅛ *small celeriac, cut into thin matchsticks*
- *juice of ¼ lemon*
- *1 tbsp crème fraîche*
- *good dollop of mayonnaise*
- *1 tsp Dijon mustard*
- *2 slices rye or sourdough bread*
- *salt and freshly ground black pepper*
- *2 slices smoked salmon*
- *2 sprigs of fresh dill (optional)*

Really quite a sophisticated sandwich. You can make the celeriac (celery root) mixture the evening before for minimum fuss and assemble the whole thing at work so you can keep the salmon refrigerated.

Add the celeriac to a small Tupperware. Squeeze over the lemon juice, mix, then add the crème fraîche, mayo, and mustard, and mix again. Cover and refrigerate.

In the morning, toast the bread while you make your coffee. Leave it to cool, and remove the celeriac mix from the fridge. Season and mix well, and put the lid back on for transporting. Wrap the salmon slices securely in parchment paper.

Separately wrap the toasted bread in parchment paper. Remember to pop the celeriac and salmon in the fridge when you get to work.

Twenty minutes before you want to eat, take everything out of the fridge, lay the salmon on a piece of bread, add the celeriac, dill (if using), and black pepper, and top with the second slice of bread. Enjoy.

EGG SALAD SANDWICH

Preparation time: 15 minutes
Makes 1 sandwich

- 2 eggs
- 1 generous tbsp mayonnaise, plus extra for spreading
- salt and freshly ground black pepper

- 2 slices bread
- 1 tomato, sliced
- handful of watercress or arugula

Never has a sandwich been so misrepresented. We don't know what the concoction most supermarkets call egg salad really is, but it tastes nothing like this.

While you're making your coffee in the morning, put a small pan of water on to boil. Once boiling, gently add the eggs (be careful, as you don't want them to crack). Set your watch/oven timer/phone for 7 minutes if you like a soft yolk, and 8 minutes if you like a firmer-set yolk.

Peel the eggs under cold running water. Slice in half lengthwise then in half again, and chop roughly. Add to a bowl with the mayonnaise and a good pinch of salt and pepper, and mix. Spread the mixture across one slice of bread. Spread a thin layer of mayo over the other. Season the egg-mayo mixture again, lightly, then add the tomato and watercress. Close together.

HUMMUS & SALAMI

Preparation time: 5 minutes at most
Makes 1 sandwich

- 2 slices brown bread
- 2 generous tbsp hummus
- 2 or 3 large slices salami
(a garlicky Italian one is ideal here)

A friend of ours swears by this sandwich, so much so in fact that—like Harriet the Spy with her tomato sandwiches—she eats it every day. Don't stinge on the hummus or it will be very dry.

S pread each side of bread generously with hummus, lay the salami on one side, sandwich together, slice, and enjoy.

THE BLT

Preparation time: 8 minutes
Makes 1 sandwich

- 2 slices bread
- 1 tsp extra-virgin olive oil
- 6 slices bacon, the best you can afford
- 2 tsp mayonnaise
- freshly ground black pepper
- 2–3 baby romaine lettuce leaves
- 1 tomato

What a beauty. Everyone has their own method—this is ours. A sort of amalgamation of hungover creativity from various friends' kitchens: we have a loud redhead to thank for the spectacularly inspired "bacon lattice," while the overwhelming addition of black pepper is taken from years of sandwiches made with love and care on sleepy weekend mornings by a half-French, half-Scottish blond.

The key here is to sandwich the tomato between the lettuce and the bacon, thus preventing Le Sog. We also prefer not to slice the whole thing in half as this could induce tomato slippage.

Very lightly toast the bread. There should barely be a hint of gold. Leave to cool on a cutting board. Heat a teaspoon of olive oil in a frying pan before adding the bacon. Cook to taste—we like ours pretty crispy.

While the bacon is crackling away, add a spoonful of mayonnaise to each slice of the cooled bread, using the back of the spoon to spread it evenly. Grind over a teaspoon of black pepper on both sides. Arrange your lettuce on one slice, carefully covering every last inch. Next, slice your tomato (you'll probably only need about half of it) and, using a paper towel, pat to soak up any excess moisture. Lay the tomato slices over the lettuce.

Remove the bacon and leave on some paper towels for a few minutes. It needs to be cool enough to handle. On the remaining slice of bread, lay three bits of bacon down in a row. Next, create the bacon lattice by "threading" the remaining bits of bacon over and under the first three slices. This will ensure a perfect bacon ratio in every bite, and stop it slipping out of the sandwich. Bliss. Cover tightly with foil. Fight the urge to eat the sandwich for breakfast.

PASTRAMI, PICKLE, SWISS & MUSTARD

Preparation time: 5 minutes
Makes 1 sandwich

- 2 slices rye bread
- generous amount of Colman's or other spicy yellow mustard
- 2 slices Swiss cheese

- 4 slices pastrami
- 1 large dill pickle, sliced thinly lengthwise

This is like a less-dirty Reuben. The mustard should clean out your sinuses.

Spread both pieces of bread with a generous amount of mustard (or less, if you don't want your eyes to water as you bite in). Lay the cheese, then the pastrami, then the pickle slices (if you start with the cheese it will act as a guard against sog). Sandwich together.

A PLOUGHMAN'S FOR THE INDOOR WORKER

Preparation time: 15 minutes
Makes 1 serving

- *generous chunk (adjust size according to hunger) of good, strong cheese*
- *2 slices ham*
- *generous helping of a relish or chutney of your choice (or whatever is left in the fridge)*
- *a couple of pickled onions/cornichons or gherkins (optional)*
- *1 small baguette/hunk of bread*
- *4 cherry or small plum tomatoes*

Perfect for a desk picnic, when you can't get outside. Add pickled onions and cornichons to the mix at your colleagues' peril.

In the morning
If you are using frozen bread, preheat your oven to 400°F.

Wrap your cheese and ham in separate parcels of parchment paper. Transfer your relish or chutney of choice into a small jam jar. Wrap any pickles you dare to bring in a small piece of foil.

Bake the bread according to the instructions (usually around 10 minutes)—until golden and crispy.

Wrap the bread in a clean dish towel, and tuck the tomatoes in. Layer everything in a bag: bread first, then the cheese and ham parcels, then the pickle and the jar. Don't forget a knife if you don't have access to one at work.

Come lunchtime
Spread everything out on the dish towel and turn on your desk lamp. Pretend you're in a café garden.

SCANDI-STYLE OPEN SANDWICHES

Preparation time: 9 minutes
Makes 1 serving

- *1 egg*
- *butter, for spreading*
- *3 slices rye bread*
- *2 slices ham or cooked beef*
- *2 slices cheese*
- *2–3 cornichons or gherkins*

- *2 cherry tomatoes*
- *2 baby romaine lettuce leaves*
- *lemon wedge*
- *sprig of fresh dill*
- *freshly ground black pepper*
- *2 slices smoked salmon*

Definitely something to assemble at work. This dish is all in the shopping and in the clever packing. Handy if you are leaving the house in a rush.

In the morning

Put a pot of water on to boil and, when boiling, add the egg and cook for 7 minutes. When ready, run under the cold tap.

Butter the 3 slices of rye bread and lay them on top of each other in a Tupperware. Cover with a sheet of parchment paper and top with all of the ingredients minus the smoked salmon and the egg. Pack the fish and boiled egg in a separate container.

Come lunchtime

Lay the 3 slices of bread on a plate, buttered sides facing up. Top the first with layers of cheese and the boiled egg, peeled and sliced into segments. Top the second with a lettuce leaf followed by rolled pieces of smoked salmon, squeezing over lemon juice and sprinkling a little pepper and dill on top. And finally, top the third piece with a lettuce leaf, the slices of meat, cornichons, and halved tomatoes. Voilà. A feast for the eyes—and the stomach.

4: FORAGING: THE CORNER OF THE CUPBOARD AND THE BACK OF THE FRIDGE

We've all been there: you come back from vacation and the only thing in the fridge is an end bit of low-fat Cheddar that was a mistake three weeks ago, and is now definitely past its best. That's dinner sorted at least, but the question remains, what are you going to have for lunch tomorrow when—horror of horrors—you have to return to work?

The skill here is to look beyond the packet of garam masala that you bought two years ago, and the dust-coated box of artisan pasta some well-meaning soul gave you for Christmas, and see the potential in the kitchen cabinet stalwarts and the fridge lurkers.

Replace canned tomatoes, beans, chickpeas, pasta, and couscous after you use them and you will be guaranteed to be able to make a nice, quickish, and inexpensive lunch next time. Add a few freezer- and fridge-friendly items to this bounty and not only will you always be able to make yourself something palatable for lunch, but you will also be able to delete the pizza delivery number from your phone, forever.

On page 18 we list the items that we find indispensable, but you should tailor these to your own tastes. If, like us, pasta with puttanesca sauce would be your final supper of choice, make sure you always (barring actual disaster) have jars of anchovies, olives, and capers. This way, you will never be caught short. Of course, sometimes disaster does strike, and you won't have these things. This is when you have to look harder: that pack of instant noodles that someone once brought round and left, or a half a bag of couscous and some tomato paste that can be transformed into something delicious, with a little bit of effort.

CANNELLINI BEAN & TUNA SALAD

Preparation time: 8 minutes (5 minutes chopping, 3 minutes to put it all together)
Makes 2 servings

- 1 can of tuna, drained
- 1 x 15 oz can cannellini beans, drained
- 1 tomato, chopped
- 1 stick celery, washed and chopped into small cubes
- ⅓ red onion, very finely chopped
- handful of fresh basil leaves
- 2 tbsp extra-virgin olive oil
- 2 tbsp balsamic vinegar

A refreshing little salad that deserves mopping up with some crusty bread.

Combine all the ingredients in your lunch container and mix well. If you can, keep refrigerated, both for the salad's sake and your colleagues'.

FORAGING: Beans and lentils (or things in cans and packets that you forget are in your kitchen cabinet)

DOUBLE BEAN SALAD

Preparation time: 15 minutes, plus overnight chilling
Makes 2 servings

- 1 x 15 oz can pinto/cannellini beans
- handful of green beans, ends cut
- ¼ red onion, finely diced
- ¼ red chili (or ½ if it is a small one), seeded and finely chopped
- ¼ garlic clove, crushed
- 1 tbsp extra-virgin olive oil
- 1 tbsp balsamic vinegar
- juice of ½ lime
- salt and freshly ground black pepper
- pita or flatbread
- a few lettuce leaves
- chopped tomato

This needs a bit of time to soak up its dressing, so it's a good idea to make it the evening before.

The night before

Boil some fresh water. While you're waiting, drain and rinse your canned beans in a colander and add to a large bowl. Once the water has boiled, add the green beans to a heatproof bowl and cover with boiling water. Put a dish towel over the top so that the steam can't escape, and leave for 3 minutes. Heat a griddle pan until smoking hot, and while waiting, drain the green beans and cut in half. Add the green beans to the pan (without any oil) and leave for 1½ minutes until they start to char (and pop). Shake and cook for another 1½ minutes before removing from the heat.

Add the chopped onion, chili, crushed garlic, oil, vinegar, and a squeeze of lime to the canned beans and mix. Season with salt and pepper, add the green beans, and mix again. Leave in the fridge overnight.

In the morning

Add to a slightly toasted pita or flatbread, with a little padding of chopped lettuce and tomato.

FORAGING: *Beans and lentils (or things in cans and packets that you forget are in your kitchen cabinet)*

CHICKPEA SALAD WITH CUMIN

Preparation time: 25 minutes (15 minutes cooking, 10 minutes cooling)
Makes 2 lunch servings or 4 side salad servings

- 1 tbsp extra-virgin olive oil
- 1 heaped tsp ground cumin
- 1 x 15 oz can chickpeas, drained
- ½ green chili
- ½ red chili
- 1 tsp whole cumin seeds
- ½ cucumber, chopped into ½ in chunks
- 8 cherry or plum tomatoes, quartered, or 1 medium tomato, chopped into ½ in chunks

- ½ red onion, finely chopped
- salt and freshly ground black pepper
- handful of parsley leaves (optional)

For the dressing
- juice of ½ lemon
- 1 tbsp extra-virgin olive oil
- 1 tbsp red wine vinegar
- salt

This salad is inspired by the delicious chickpeas at Moro and Morito in Exmouth Market, London. If you don't have fresh chili, do not despair: a small sprinkling of dried chili flakes will still work well.

Add the oil to a pan and put it on the heat. While the pan is warming, place the ground cumin in a large bowl. Add the drained chickpeas in large spoonfuls, shaking the bowl about in between spoons to make sure that all the chickpeas are evenly coated. Add to the pan (you may want to check first that it is sufficiently hot by throwing a test chickpea in and seeing if it sizzles) and season before leaving to cook for 5 minutes, stirring occasionally. Keep an eye on the heat: you want them to crisp up but not burn. Seed and chop your chilies and add to the pan, leaving to cook for a further few minutes.

Take the chickpeas off the heat, place in a large bowl and, once cool, sprinkle over the cumin seeds.

Now make the dressing: squeeze the lemon juice into a jam jar, then add the oil and vinegar and a pinch of salt and shake.

When packing, if you are in a hurry you can transfer the chopped cucumber, tomato, red onion, and chilis into one Tupperware and the chickpeas into another and assemble these plus the dressing at lunchtime. If not, then simply add the salad to the chickpeas once they are fully cool.

Come lunchtime
Add the dressing and parsley, if using, just before eating, and mix well.

LEMON & CILANTRO DAHL

Preparation time: 5 minutes, plus 35 minutes cooking
Makes 2–3 servings

- 1–2 tbsp butter
- 1 tbsp extra-virgin olive oil
- 2 medium white onions
- ½ tsp ground cumin
- ½ tsp ras el hanout
- 1 tsp ground coriander
- 1 tsp cayenne pepper
- 3½ oz yellow split peas (soaked overnight in water)
- 1¾ oz red lentils
- 3 cups fresh water
- thumb-sized piece of ginger, grated
- 2 garlic cloves, crushed
- salt
- 3 carrots
- juice of 2 lemons
- 3 tbsp chopped fresh cilantro

This is delicious all year round and one that we enjoy serving again and again to our vegetarian friends. The fresh lemon juice and cilantro added at the end really lift this dish.

Put a heavy-bottomed pan on a medium heat and add the butter and olive oil. Finely chop the onions and add to the pan. Leave to soften for a few minutes, then add the spices. Mix for a minute or two before adding the drained split peas and lentils, and continue stirring until everything is nicely covered in the onions and spices.

Add the water, grated ginger, crushed garlic, and salt, then bring to a boil. Lower the heat to a simmer, and leave the lentils and peas to cook for about half an hour. If the pan starts to get a little dry, add some more water and put a lid on the pan.

About 15 minutes before the end of the cooking time, peel and chop the carrots and add to the dish.

When the carrots are tender and the lentils and peas are cooked, turn the heat off and leave to cool with the lid on.

Blend the soup to your liking using a handheld blender (we like ours to stay a bit chunky with some whole lentils and bits of carrot). Add the lemon juice, chopped cilantro, and taste to check the seasoning.

Come lunchtime
Enjoy reheated with some rice or simply on its own.

WHOLE WHEAT PASTA WITH
BROAD BEANS & BACON

....

Preparation time: 40 minutes
Makes 1 serving

- *1 tbsp extra-virgin olive oil, plus extra for drizzling*
- *3 slices of bacon*
- *2 cups frozen broad (fava) beans*
- *3½ oz whole wheat penne pasta*
- *2 tsp freshly ground black pepper*
- *2 tbsp grated Parmesan*
- *salt*

....

*B*road beans and bacon are a classic Spanish combination. The addition of whole wheat pasta here makes this dish a little more substantial.

....

The night before

Fill a small pot or saucepan with 4 cups fresh water and put it on to boil. Put another pot of salted water on a high heat for the pasta. Heat the olive oil in a small frying pan on a medium to high heat. Add the bacon to the pan, using scissors to snip into small chunks. Cook until nice and crispy before draining and cooling on a paper towel.

When the fresh water has boiled, pour the 4 cups of water into a large heatproof bowl. Add the frozen broad beans and leave to defrost until the water has completely cooled, about 15 minutes.

Meanwhile, cook the pasta according to the package instructions in the other pot of boiling water. Once cooked, drain and pop into your Tupperware container.

Drizzle over a little olive oil, add the black pepper and bacon, along with the grated Parmesan and mix well.

Now comes the tedious bit; we recommend doing this next part while watching an episode of whatever's flavor of the month on TV. Take the now tepid bowl of broad beans and fish them out one by one. Give them a squeeze to slide the bright inner beans out of their dull "shells" and put to one side. An oddly satisfying, mindless task akin to finishing one's expenses.

Stir the bright green broad beans into your pasta dish and pop in the fridge.

Come lunchtime

Enjoy either at room temperature or reheated.

FORAGING: *Superfoods, or pasta and other dried carbs*

BROCCOLI, ANCHOVY
& CHILI ORECCHIETTE

Preparation time: 20 minutes
Makes 1 serving

- *good splash of extra-virgin olive oil*
- *1 garlic clove, sliced*
- *2 anchovy fillets*
- *pinch of dried chili flakes (optional)*

- *2½ oz orecchiette/pasta of your choice*
- *9 oz frozen broccoli*
- *pinch of salt*

*L*ike puttanesca, this is another of our favorite kitchen cabinet recipes: it is cheap, uses very few ingredients, and is even quicker to make than its tomato-based relative. We like to use orecchiette, as the bashed-up ears get nicely coated, but you can use any shape you like. Frozen broccoli is a wonderful thing: keep some in your freezer, always.

In the morning

Fill a large pot with water, add salt and put on to boil. Add olive oil to a separate pan and gently cook the garlic, taking care not to let it burn. After a minute add the anchovies, breaking them down in the pan with the back of a spoon. Once they're disintegrated, add the chili flakes and turn off the heat.

Once the water is boiling, add the pasta. Cook for 4 minutes before adding the broccoli to the same pot—cook for a further 5 minutes. When the pasta is al dente and the broccoli cooked through, drain them, saving a small amount of the cooking water in a mug. Roughly chop the broccoli, then add both pasta and broccoli to the pan of garlic and anchovy, and cook on a low heat for around 3 minutes, adding a splash of cooking water to amalgamate. Transfer to your lunch pail or Tupperware.

Come lunchtime

Enjoy either slightly warmed or at room temperature. If you're not reheating, then don't refrigerate it—these little shells have a nasty habit of sticking to each other.

WHOLE WHEAT PASTA WITH ZUCCHINI

Preparation time: 15 minutes
Makes 1 serving

- *1 portion of whole wheat pasta*
- *4 tsp extra-virgin olive oil*
- *1 garlic clove, chopped*
- *1 zucchini, peeled into ribbons, or if you own the same gadget as us, sliced into spaghetti strands*
- *salt and freshly ground black pepper*
- *juice of ½ lemon*
- *handful of grated Parmesan*
- *1 tbsp chopped fresh chives*
- *1 or 2 sprigs of dill*

We've recently invested in a kitchen gadget which creates spaghetti-like strands from vegetables such as zucchini; the idea being to cook carb-free pasta recipes. While we're not quite ready to give up eating pasta, we have been enjoying new, possibly unlikely combinations of ingredients in our dishes, like this one.

In the morning

Put a pot of salted water on the heat, and once boiling, add the pasta. While it's cooking, heat 2 teaspoons of olive oil in a small pan on a low heat and sauté the garlic, taking care not to burn it.

Add the zucchini, sprinkle with salt and pepper and a little of the lemon juice and turn the heat up, cooking for 1 minute, until just slightly softened.

Once the pasta is cooked, drain and add to your lunch receptacle, stirring in the remaining olive oil and lemon juice, Parmesan, and salt and pepper. Taste and adjust the seasoning if necessary. Stir the zucchini into the pasta and sprinkle over the chives and dill.

Come lunchtime

This is best enjoyed at room temperature.

TOMATO COUSCOUS

Preparation time: 30 minutes
Makes 2 servings

- 2 tbsp extra-virgin olive oil
- ½ red or white onion, thinly sliced
- 1 garlic clove, finely sliced
- ½ chicken stock cube
- 2 large tomatoes or 8 small tomatoes, chopped
- salt and freshly ground black pepper
- ½ tsp sugar
- ¼ tsp ground cinnamon
- very generous spoonful of tomato paste
- 5 oz couscous
- 1 tbsp unsalted butter

It can only be the butter that makes this so good. This makes too much for one serving, but you'll be glad of it when you wearily open the fridge after work.

Boil the water for your cup of tea or your cafetière if you are a sophisticated coffee person (we aspire to be you). Add the oil to a pan on a low heat and add the sliced onion and garlic. Leave to soften, stirring occasionally, making sure they do not color.

Add boiling water to the stock cube to make ½ to ⅔ cup of stock. Cover with a dish towel.

Place the tomatoes in a plastic bowl, and pour enough boiling water over to completely cover their tops. Leave for a couple of minutes. Remove and peel off the skin, which should come away easily. Slice into quarters and chop into small diced pieces. Add to the onion and garlic in the pan, along with the salt and pepper, sugar, cinnamon, and tomato paste. Cook on a medium heat for 5 minutes until the tomatoes start to break down.

Turn off the heat, and add the dried couscous to the pan. Add the stock and butter and swiftly stir, then cover the pan with a dish towel—make sure the stove is turned off! Leave for 5 minutes, then taste and season again if necessary. Transfer to your lunch pail and seal securely.

Come lunchtime
Enjoy at room temperature with a few crunchy lettuce leaves and a dressing of oil and lemon.

FORAGING: Superfoods, or pasta and other dried carbs

PARMA HAM & TOMATO PASTA

Preparation time: 15 minutes
Makes 1 serving

- 1 large tomato
- 1 tbsp extra-virgin olive oil, plus extra for drizzling
- 1 garlic clove, finely chopped
- ½ tsp chili flakes
- salt and freshly ground black pepper
- 1 portion of pasta
- 3 slices cured ham (Parma or iberico are lovely)
- grated Parmesan (optional)

This is barely a recipe. Just a combination of some of our favorite things: good-quality Parma ham, a delicious tomato sauce made from fresh tomato, and pasta. Baby food really.

Place a pot of salted water on to boil, lid on. Chop the tomato into small pieces, discarding some of the seeds if there are lots. In a small frying pan, heat the olive oil and add the garlic, tomato, and chili flakes. Sprinkle over some salt and cook for 2 minutes.

When the water in the pot is boiling, add the pasta and cook according to the package instructions. Meanwhile, slice your cured ham. When the pasta is ready, drain and add to your lunch container. Pour over the garlicky tomato "sauce," with a little extra olive oil and pepper, then top with the chopped ham and grated Parmesan, if using.

Come lunchtime
Mix well and enjoy at room temperature.

POOR MAN'S PAELLA

Preparation time: 35 minutes
Makes 1 generous serving

- 2 tbsp extra-virgin olive oil
- ½ red onion, sliced into chunky strips
- 1 garlic clove, sliced
- ½ red pepper, seeded and sliced (optional)
- salt and freshly ground black pepper
- ¼ tsp smoked paprika
- ¼ tsp turmeric
- ¼ tsp chili flakes

- large handful of sliced chorizo (optional)
- 2½ oz Arborio rice
- ½ chicken stock cube
- 5 cherry or small tomatoes, roughly chopped
- handful of roughly chopped fresh parsley (optional)
- lemon wedge

This creation is inspired by the Vegetable Paella in Plenty. Like so many others, we blame Ottolenghi for our luxe food habits, although this annotated version was conceived when we didn't have most (okay, basically, all) of the ingredients called for in the original. It just shows how good the recipe is when, stripped back to its bare bones like this, it still tastes fantastic. You really don't need much to make it, just a few cabinet and fridge lurkers. Frozen peas would be a welcome addition, if you have them.

Add the oil to a frying pan until hot, then add the chopped onion, garlic, and pepper. Fry for 5 minutes, until it starts to soften and slightly color, then, add salt and pepper and the spices. Fry for 3 more minutes, before adding the chorizo, if using, and the rice. Put 1 cup of water on to boil for the chicken stock while you stir and fry for a further 3 minutes. Make up the chicken stock, add to the pan and turn down to the lowest possible heat. Put a lid on the pan and leave for around 20 minutes, adding the tomatoes after 15 minutes. If it looks like it's drying out, then add a splash more water. Taste the rice to make sure it's cooked. When soft, season again if necessary, transfer to your lunch container, and leave to cool. It's best enjoyed at room temperature, so don't refrigerate.

Come lunchtime
Before eating, sprinkle with parsley and squeeze a generous amount of lemon juice over the top.

FORAGING: Superfoods, or pasta and other dried carbs

JUST ADD WATER . . .

*E*ven *if your office is the kind of barren wasteland where removing your tea bag from your mug with a ballpoint pen is the norm, it should, god-willing, have a way to heat water. These recipes simply involve adding boiling water at the office before eating. Think of them as chic Cup-a-Soups.*

JAPANESE BROTH

Preparation time: 5 minutes in the morning, then a few minutes at work
Makes 1 serving

- *2 baby leeks*
- *1 mushroom*
- *1 small carrot*

- *dry rice vermicelli noodles*
- *miso soup packet*
- *soy sauce (optional)*

A packet of miso paste provides the base for this simple broth.

Slice the leeks lengthwise down the middle, fan open, and rinse well under the cold tap to remove any grit. Then cut in half, before slicing as finely as possible (aiming for strips as thin as spaghetti strands). Pop in a large heat-proof container or jar, along with the mushroom after slicing. Trim the carrot, and peel into ribbons before adding to the mix along with the noodles. Pop the miso soup packet on top and seal your container.

Come lunchtime
Put the kettle on or use the microwave to boil fresh water. Fish out the packet from your jar, and if using a bowl, squeeze out the miso into it, along with the other ingredients.

Pour over the boiling water and, using a fork, "whisk" the soup until the miso has dissolved. Leave the soup to rest for 2 minutes before enjoying. If you have some soy sauce at the office, a dash here would work well.

SOUTHEAST ASIAN PHO

Preparation time: 6 minutes in the morning, then a few minutes at work
Makes 1 serving

- thumb-sized piece of ginger
- ½ red chili
- 3 scallions
- ½ yellow pepper
- 2 handfuls of spinach
- 2 oz vermicelli rice noodles

- ½ chicken/vegetable stock cube (or a generous pinch of salt)
- 1 lime
- handful of cilantro and basil (Thai sweet basil would be ideal)

A tasty tribute to the Gap Yahs of old, this simple soup can be made with pretty much any vegetable you'd eat raw. Adjust the chili quantity according to your spice tolerance level.

If your office isn't stocked with a soup bowl, peel the ginger and grate into a large heatproof jar or container. Finely chop the chili and add to the minced ginger. Slice the scallions and pepper, and pop inside too. Add the spinach leaves and rice noodles, along with the stock cube fragment. Slice the lime in half and pop inside, then finely chop the herbs and add to the mix.

Come lunchtime
Put the kettle on or use the microwave to boil fresh water. Fish out the lime from your jar, and if using a bowl, transfer the ingredients into it. Pour over the boiling water and, using a fork, "whisk" the soup until the stock has dissolved. If you are going to eat from your jar, fill it up to two thirds of the way, close the lid and give it a good shake. Leave the soup to rest for a minute or two before squeezing over the lime juice from the two halves. Enjoy.

FORAGING: *Just add water...*

DONE-UP INSTANT NOODLES

Preparation time: 5 minutes in the morning, 5 minutes at work
Makes 1 serving

- 1 scallion, finely chopped
- ½ red chili, seeded and finely chopped
- 4–5 leaves bok choi (Chinese cabbage), roughly chopped
- splash of soy sauce
- splash of fish sauce
- 1 packet instant noodles
- ½ lime

Everyone has a variation on instant noodles in their kitchen cabinet, whether it's Top Ramen, or those exotic packs with a photo of an egg and a shrimp on the front that you can buy in Asian supermarkets for 50 cents. If it's the latter, then they're normally pretty nice as they are, but here are a few tips for jazzing (and freshening) them up. Adding a bit of greenery elevates this to something acceptable for consumption in the workplace, instead of at 7 a.m., under your comforter, crying. This is the ultimate grab-and-go lunch: you do all the assembling at work.

In the morning

Once you've done all your chopping transfer the scallion, chili, and bok choi to a small Tupperware. Keeping some soy and fish sauce at work is convenient, and useful for enlivening lackluster lunches, but if you'd rather not, then just add a couple of splashes to a small jam jar.

Come lunchtime

Add the dried noodles to a bowl—a large mug will do at a pinch if you don't have a bowl. If they look nice, add some of the little packets of sauce that come with your noodles. Add enough hot water (from your office water dispenser or using the microwave will do) to cover the noodles. Cover your bowl/mug with a clean dish towel or piece of paper towel, to keep the steam in. Leave for 3 minutes. Add the soy-fish sauce combo, and sprinkle in the chopped ingredients. Chili oil is also a good addition if you like things fiery. Squeeze in the lime juice. Stir. Enjoy.

If you have 5 minutes to spare in the morning, fry the scallion with a tiny bit of oil until charred.

SPICY LENTIL & COCONUT SOUP

Preparation time: 10 minutes, plus 40 minutes cooking
Makes 2 servings

- *1 tbsp extra-virgin olive oil*
- *1 tbsp red curry paste*
- *1 onion, finely chopped*
- *1 carrot, finely chopped*
- *1 cup of your preferred combination of red*
- *and green lentils (yellow split peas also work well, but you must have the foresight to soak them beforehand)*
- *1 x 14 oz can coconut milk*
- *½ tsp salt*

The kitchen cabinet forager's favorite. This delicious soup involves just two fresh ingredients: a carrot and an onion.

Take a medium-sized, heavy-bottomed casserole and pop on a medium to low heat. Add the olive oil and after a minute, the curry paste. Stir well and leave to heat through. Add the onion to the pan and stir for a minute or two. Add the chopped carrot (you won't purée this soup, so make sure your carrot chunks are nice and small) to the cooking onions.

Add in the cup of lentils, stirring well to coat with all the spices for a minute or two before pouring over the coconut milk. Fill the empty can with water and add the contents to the pan. Then fill it again to about halfway and add to the pan.

Add the salt and then bring to a boil. Lower the heat and simmer for 40 minutes. Transfer to a thermos.

PEA & MINT SOUP

Preparation time: 20 minutes

Makes 2 servings

- 1–2 tbsp butter
- 1 tbsp extra-virgin olive oil, plus extra for drizzling if serving cold
- ½ onion, chopped
- 1 stick celery, chopped into small chunks (so that it cooks more quickly)
- 9 oz frozen petit pois
- 1¼ cups vegetable stock/bouillon
- salt and freshly ground black pepper
- generous handful of mint, stalks and all, washed and chopped

A summery soup classic and just as nice chilled as it is hot—perfect for the microwave- and thermos-free luncher.

Melt the butter and oil in a pot, then add the onion and celery and sweat until soft (for around 6 minutes), taking care not to let them color. Add the frozen peas, stock, salt, and pepper and bring to a simmer, until the peas are soft (another 4 minutes).

Remove from the heat, add the chopped mint and, using a hand blender, purée the ingredients. Check the seasoning and consistency, adding more salt and pepper and a splash of water if necessary. If serving cold, drizzle an extra tablespoon of oil over the soup before tucking in.

PEA, FETA & CHILI FRITTATA

Preparation time: 15 minutes
Makes 1 serving

- ½ tbsp extra-virgin olive oil
- 3 generous tbsp frozen peas
- 2 eggs

- salt and freshly ground black pepper
- 2 tbsp crumbled feta
- ¼ red chili, seeded and finely chopped

It's tempting to eat this spicy and salty frittata as soon as it's out of the pan. But if you do that then you won't have any lunch left.

Turn on the broiler. Heat the oil in a small ovenproof pan and, once warm, add the peas. Crack the eggs into a bowl and whisk, then add salt and pepper. Add the crumbled feta and chili and mix. Turn up the heat on the pan, then pour in the egg mix. Cook for 5 minutes, then transfer the pan to the broiler, and leave for a further 5 minutes or until top is lightly golden. Remove carefully and leave to cool.

Slice into wedges and store in a Tupperware or tiffin tin until you're ready to eat. A few crispy leaves are a good accompaniment.

WHEN YOU RUN OUT OF BREAD . . .
ALWAYS KEEP SOME PITA IN THE FREEZER

Think of pita as a bread-based accessory: Like Mary Poppins's never-ending tapestry bag, a humble pita can pack in a deceptive amount. It is relatively sturdy, providing you are careful with your use of condiments, which makes it an excellent lunch conveyer. It is cheap, readily available at even the most basic corner shop, and a dream to store. We always freeze ours as, frankly, who would dream of eating an untoasted pita? To heap more praise on to its wheaty shoulders, it is far healthier and more portable than its cousin, the wrap. When our kitchen cabinets are at their most bare, we can usually find a pita knocking around our tiny freezers, and thank god for that.

Prepping your pita
Do this while waiting for your cup of tea or coffee, or waiting for the shower to get warm. It doesn't matter if it cools down as you're not going to eat it hot—just make sure that it doesn't burn, as the more toasted and hard it becomes, the less malleable and harder to fill it will be. Toast and, once cool, slide the tip of a sharp knife into the edge of the wide side of the pita, carefully sliding it round. Jiggle it a little if necessary to ensure that the cavity is as deep as possible, taking care not to make any holes in the bread.

Packing your pita
The pita is a versatile thing, but it benefits from close wrapping. We would recommend tightly wrapping in foil (the firm texture of the foil helps it to keep its shape) or, if in a pinch, a double layer of plastic wrap, for added tightness, will do.

Filling your pita—9 ideas
All the following go very nicely indeed in a pita. If you feel like more salad, you can pad the bottom out with some chopped lettuce, tomato, and cucumber, add your filling of choice, and finish off with more salad on top.

• Tuna with basil and capers (see page 86)
• Double bean salad (see page 101)
• Ready-made falafels, squashed, with hummus or tzatziki and chili sauce
• Paul Missing's special chickpeas (see page 140)
• Chickpea salad with cumin (see page 102)
• Rainbow rescue (see page 31)
• Avocado salad (see page 26)
• Chickpea, Parmesan and red onion salad (see page 29)
• Cannellini bean and tuna salad (see page 100)

PISSALADIÈRE

Preparation time: 35–40 minutes
Makes enough to share, or have leftovers

- ⅓ sheet ready-rolled puff pastry
- 3 tbsp extra-virgin olive oil
- 1 large onion, thinly sliced
- spoonful of butter
- 1 heaping tbsp dark brown sugar

- salt and freshly ground black pepper
- leaves from 2 sprigs thyme
- 6 anchovies
- 6 oil-cured black olives
- milk, for brushing the pastry edges

As delicious a lunch as you will ever eat. As long as you're not running too late, it is actually possible to make this before you leave the house in the morning, without arriving at work with pieces of onion in your hair (it's a good thing to make when you've had an early night and feel rested). Delicious on its own or with some lettuce on the side.

First things first—and by that we mean before you even start the coffee pot—turn on your oven to 400°F and remove the puff pastry from the fridge, unwrapping it from its packaging but not, of course, unrolling it.

Add the oil to a pan, place on a medium heat and add the onions. You want them to become mushy and a deep golden-brown color, but at the same time, if you're making this in the morning, you don't want to hang around, so keep them on a medium to high heat (but take care that they don't burn). Stir occasionally with a wooden spoon.
Tip: *when you're not using the spoon, don't leave it in the pan. As a chef once said to us, "you don't want to cook the spoon."*

Add the butter, sugar, and salt and pepper and stir. Adding a splash or two of water will help to prevent the onions

burning and creates a saucy consistency. Add the thyme, and leave to cook for 15 minutes, again making sure that the onions don't burn and adding more water if necessary.

Carefully unroll a section of the sheet of puff pastry and, using scissors, cut the section away from the rest of the roll, through the pastry and the paper it comes on, the same way you would cut off a piece of wrapping paper. Keep the rectangle of pastry on the paper. Now, choose the receptacle that you are going to use to transport the tart (square or rectangular Tupperware or tin would be ideal) and place it face down on the pastry. Using a sharp knife, cut around the edge, discarding the extra pastry. Fold over each of the sides of the pastry by ½ in (going towards the inside), so that you create a ridged edge around the outside of the tart. Transfer your tart to a baking tray, and poke the base with a fork—this will stop the middle bit rising. You want the edges to rise to create a crust, so don't poke those.

When your onions are nice and soft, take off the heat and spoon the mixture on to your pastry base, taking care not to go over the edge of the border. Smooth it with a knife so that the surface is evenly covered. Place your anchovies on the top in a lattice or criss-cross pattern, adding the olives in between the diamonds. Brush the edges of the pastry with milk, and bake for 12 minutes, until the pastry is crisp and golden.

Packing your pastry
You can simply wrap your tart in lots of foil, put it in a bag and hope for the best, but you will have a stressful (though delicious smelling) journey to work. Better to use the roomy Tupperware that you used to measure your pastry size and line it with enough parchment paper that you can fold it over the top of the tart once it is placed inside. Structure is good for your tart.

Feta and red onion variation
A delicious variation on the above: Prepare the pastry and onions—minus the thyme—as directed above. At the end, omit the olives and anchovies and instead crumble over some feta and then sprinkle over the thyme. Cook for the same amount of time.

TOMATO, PESTO & GOAT CHEESE TART

Preparation time: 5 minutes, plus 5 minutes cooking time. Makes 1 serving

- ⅓ sheet ready-rolled puff pastry
- 1 tsp pesto
- 1 tomato, sliced
- handful of crumbled mild goat cheese
- ½ tsp dried thyme
- milk, for brushing the pastry edges
- green salad, to serve

For the salad dressing
- ½ tbsp extra-virgin olive oil
- splash of red wine vinegar
- 1 tsp Dijon mustard
- salt and freshly ground black pepper

As with the Pissaladière, preheat the oven to 400°F and take the puff pastry out of the fridge. Remove it from its packaging, but wait at least 10 minutes before unrolling it.

Meanwhile prepare the other ingredients: wash and pack your green salad, and prepare the salad dressing in a small Tupperware or mini jam jar. Nestle the dressing container into your salad container like a Russian doll.

Carefully unwrap a section of the sheet of puff pastry and, using scissors, cut the section away from the rest of the roll, through the pastry and the paper, the same way you would cut off a piece of wrapping paper. Keep the rectangle of pastry on the paper it came on. Now, choose the receptacle that you are going to use to transport the tart (square or rectangular Tupperware would be ideal) and place it face down on the pastry. Using a sharp knife cut around the receptacle, discarding the extra pastry. Fold over each of the sides of the pastry by ½ in (going toward the inside), so that you create a ridged edge around the

outside of the tart. Transfer your tart to a baking tray, and poke the base with a fork—this will stop the middle bit rising. You want the edges to rise to create a crust, so don't poke those.

Coat the base with 1 teaspoon of pesto and layer the tomato slices on top. Crumble over a generous amount of goat cheese and sprinkle over the thyme.

Brush the edges of the pastry with milk, and bake for 12 minutes, until the pastry is crisp and golden. It should fit perfectly in the Tupperware container you used to cut its edge.

Come lunchtime
Pour the dressing over your salad. The tart is delicious either reheated or at room temperature.

Leftover ratatouille or roasted vegetables of any kind are delicious on puff pastry tarts. Simply spoon over the cooked vegetables (e.g., roasted zucchini, eggplant, carrots even), crumble over some feta and bake as directed above. Delicious and oh so easy.

THE ENID BLYTON

Preparation time: 10 minutes
Makes 1 serving

- 2 eggs
- 2 slices bread
- softened butter
- watercress
- *Maldon sea salt*
- *freshly ground black pepper*
- *handful of radishes*
- *ginger beer (optional)*

No one did the packed lunch quite like Enid Blyton in her novels. This is our tribute: a reminder that a picnic lunch doesn't have to be complicated to be delicious. Enjoy outdoors, preferably.

In the morning

Bring a pot of water to a boil and add the eggs, leaving to cook for 7 minutes. Meanwhile, butter your bread and wash and dry the watercress. Pick the little round leaves off, discarding the bigger stalks, and place on one of the upturned slices of bread. If the butter is unsalted, sprinkle over a pinch of salt and close the sandwich with the other half.

Slice into quarters and wrap in foil. When the eggs are ready, run them under the cold tap and wrap individually in foil or together in a clean dish towel. Wash the radishes and place in a container. Pop a teaspoon of sea salt into a mini jam jar or another small Tupperware container (or grab a salt and pepper packet if you have them handy), and bring along a paper towel.

Come lunchtime

Peel your boiled eggs and sprinkle the sea salt and pepper on to the paper towel. Dip the radishes and eggs into it and enjoy, along with your outrageously old-fashioned sandwich.

5: COOKING THE NIGHT BEFORE

Time is often of the essence, as the current popularity of books on how to cook dinner in an ever-decreasing number of minutes shows. However, sometimes it's nice and soothing to set aside an hour or so in the evening and, without rushing, weave making lunch for the following day into your dinner process. Turn on the radio, pour a not ungenerous glass of wine, crush some garlic, and decompress.

The benefit of doing this is twofold, as some recipes just taste better the next day, after they've had time to sit and absorb their flavors—puttanesca or spicy chickpeas being two prime examples. But cooking the night before also means that you have little to no preparation to do in the morning before leaving for work, so it can be good time management for when you are especially busy.

ORZO PASTA SALAD

Preparation time: 30 minutes
Makes 1 generous serving

- 1 red pepper, seeded and sliced into long thin strips
- extra-virgin olive oil, for drizzling
- salt and freshly ground black pepper
- 2½ oz orzo pasta

- 8 cherry tomatoes, halved
- small handful (around 9) black olives, sliced
- 1 oz feta, crumbled into small chunks
- small handful of mint leaves
- small handful of basil leaves

*T*his isn't particularly tricky to make, but it tastes much better the following day when all the ingredients have had a chance to mingle. If you can't find orzo you can use any small pasta.

The night before

Preheat your oven to 475°F and put a small pot of salted water on to boil. Lay the pepper slices in a baking dish, drizzle with oil and salt, and cook for 15 minutes. While the peppers are cooking and once the water is boiling, cook your pasta according to the package instructions, taking care not to overcook it and draining it as soon as it's done.

Remove the tray of peppers and add the tomatoes to it, giving it a good shake (and adding a tiny bit more oil if necessary) before returning to the oven for a further 8 minutes.

Transfer the drained pasta to the dish of tomatoes and peppers (mixing it together with the juices they have produced while cooking). Leave to cool for 5 minutes then add the olives and feta, season to taste, and mix well.

In the morning

Wrap the herbs in a clean dish towel, lightly sprinkled with water, and pack on top of the Tupperware of pasta.

Come lunchtime

Snip and mix the herbs into the pasta just before eating, so they stay fresh.

PAUL MISSING'S SPECIAL CHICKPEAS

Preparation time: 45 minutes
Makes 1 serving, with more than enough for leftovers

- 1 x 15 oz can chickpeas
- 1½ tbsp extra-virgin olive oil
- sea salt and freshly ground black pepper
- 3 slices eggplant, about 1 in thick
- ½ tsp smoked paprika, plus an extra pinch to season
- ½ onion, finely chopped
- 1 large garlic clove, chopped
- ½ tsp dried chili flakes

- ½ tsp ground cumin
- ¼ tsp Chinese five-spice powder
- 1 tbsp fish sauce
- 4 tbsp chopped tomatoes (if using fresh tomatoes remove the skins)
- ½ tsp sugar or honey
- handful of freshly chopped parsley or cilantro
- 1 tsp grated lemon zest (optional)

Sophie's dad's recipe is the result of years of tireless testing. Similar to a dry curry, the aromatic, spicy chickpeas benefit from slow cooking and taste better the next day, when all the flavors have had the chance to absorb.

The night before

Preheat the oven to 350°F. Empty the can of chickpeas and brine into a medium-sized pot (adding a little water if the liquid does not just cover the chickpeas in the pot). Bring to a boil and simmer for 5 minutes, removing from the heat when the chickpeas are softened. Drain, reserving some of the cooking liquid.

Use ½ tablespoon of oil to brush both sides of the eggplant, then season with sea salt, pepper, and a pinch of smoked paprika. Place in a baking tray or dish and bake for 20 minutes, checking and turning after 10 minutes. When browned and soft, remove, then cover and set aside.

Add the remaining olive oil to a pan, and slowly cook the onion and garlic over a medium-low heat. When the onions turn translucent add the chili flakes, paprika, cumin, and five-spice powder. Cook for a minute on a low heat, then add the fish sauce and leave for a further minute before adding the chopped tomatoes and sugar or honey. Allow the tomatoes to break down—taste at this point and adjust the seasoning to your taste.

Increase the heat and cook until the liquid has reduced and the sauce resembles a dry curry. At this point add 2 tablespoons (or more if you like) of the chickpea cooking liquid you set aside earlier. Continue cooking to reduce the liquid. Taste—it should be aromatic and sweet with a pleasantly spicy finish. Add the chickpeas to the sauce and continue to cook on a low heat, turning them and incorporating them into the mixture every so often. They should be coated in sauce, but shouldn't appear wet. If they do, cook for a little longer until the liquid has reduced.

Cut the eggplant slices in half, then cut each half into 3 pieces. Add to the chickpeas and gently fold into the mixture.

Remove from the heat, add the chopped fresh parsley or cilantro, and gently mix through. Add the grated lemon rind.

In the morning
Transfer your desired portion into a Tupperware with some green leaves, or in a pita bread with some salad. The chickpeas will keep for up to a week in a sealed container in the fridge.

PUTTANESCA

Preparation time: 12 minutes, then 40 minutes of simmering
Makes 4 servings

- 2 tbsp extra-virgin olive oil
- 3 garlic cloves, finely chopped
- 2 tsp chili flakes
- 5 anchovies
- 1 x 14½ oz can chopped tomatoes
- 4 tbsp tomato paste

- 1 x 1 lb can passata (tomato purée)
- 1 tbsp capers
- 1 small can of pitted black olives*
- 1 portion of pasta of your choice
- handful of grated Cheddar or Parmesan (optional)

Quite simply the most delicious pasta sauce of all time: the trick is to make a big batch, as you will want to keep eating this day after day.

The night before
Put 2 tablespoons of olive oil in a heavy-bottomed pan on a medium to low heat. Add the finely chopped garlic, chili flakes, and anchovies. This bit is absolutely pivotal. The garlic must not burn—you just want to dissolve the anchovies into a paste. So keep an eagle eye on the pan, stirring the mixture with a wooden spoon to prevent any sticking.

When you're satisfied that the anchovies no longer resemble anchovies, quickly add the canned tomatoes . . . and breathe. Add the tomato paste and passata, along with the capers and olives.

Simmer gently for 40–60 minutes with the lid off. Once it's done, simply put the lid on and go to bed.

In the morning
Put a pot of salted water on to boil. They say if you're cooking pasta, the water should be as salty as the Mediterranean. Interpret that as you will. Cook a portion of pasta according to the package instructions. Drain and add to a container, spooning over the puttanesca sauce and mixing. Pack this container in your bag and stop to consider whether you might want to bring some grated Cheddar or Parmesan with you. It's a bit wrong, but sometimes very right.

Come lunchtime
This dish is best stored out of the fridge—it's delicious at room temperature or reheated.

* While some people prefer their olives whole, others chop them up. You can buy chopped and pitted black olives to save you the trouble, but they are a little more expensive.

COOKING THE NIGHT BEFORE: *Tastes better the next day*

EGGPLANT & TOMATO GRATIN

Preparation time: 15 minutes, plus 1 hour total cooking time
Makes 2 servings

- 1 eggplant
- 1 tbsp extra-virgin olive oil, plus extra for brushing
- 1 small onion, finely chopped
- 1 x 14 oz can tomatoes
- 1 x 14 oz can of passata (tomato purée)

- 2 garlic cloves, crushed
- large pinch of dried oregano
- ½ tsp dried thyme
- 1 tsp sugar
- handful of grated Parmesan

This is a slightly healthier take on the popular Italian dish Melanzane Parmigiana. We omit the usual half ton of mozzarella here, preferring instead a sprinkling of strong cheese over the top.

Preheat the oven to 350°F. Slice your eggplant lengthwise, about ¼ inch thick, and brush both sides of each slice with olive oil. Lay them down in a large baking tray, being careful not to overlap with one another (think Koh Tao, not Costa del Sol), and bake until golden—about 20 minutes.

Meanwhile, make your tomato sauce. Add a tablespoon of olive oil to a saucepan on a medium heat. Add the onion and soften for a few minutes. Add the can of tomatoes, followed by the passata, crushed garlic, herbs, and sugar. Leave to simmer for 20–25 minutes. Once it has reduced, taste and

adjust the seasoning.

Take a small pie or oven dish and place a layer of the cooked eggplant slices at the bottom—some overlapping is fine. Spoon over some sauce, then add the next layer of eggplant slices. Repeat until you have run out of eggplant and spoon over the remaining sauce on the top, followed by a generous helping of Parmesan. Bake in the oven for 30 minutes.

Come lunchtime
This is delicious at room temperature or reheated and works well with a green salad and a simple French garlic dressing.

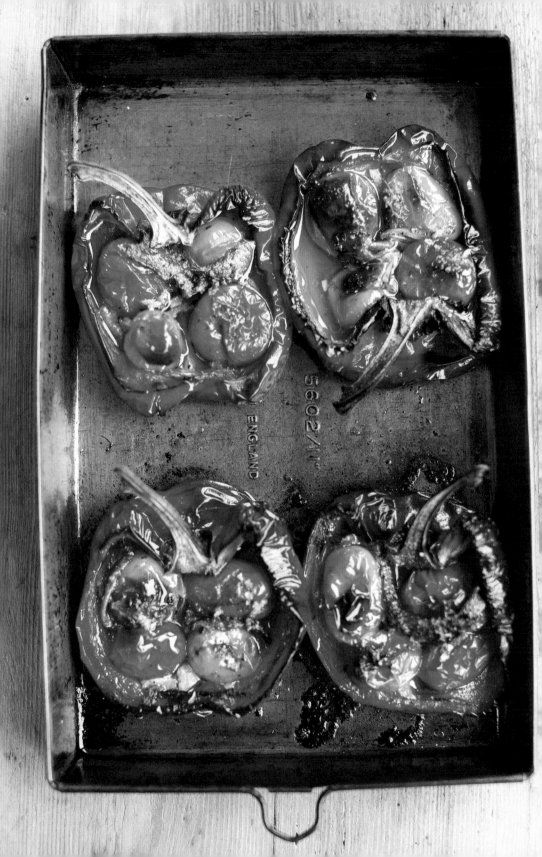

ROASTED RED PEPPERS WITH ANCHOVY & TOMATO

Preparation time: 4 minutes, plus 30 minutes cooking
Makes 1 serving (for a hungry person), with leftovers

- *2 red peppers*
- *16 cherry tomatoes*
- *4 anchovies*

- *1 garlic clove, sliced*
- *extra-virgin olive oil, for drizzling*

This recipe is easy and requires very few ingredients. Delicious served with bread or couscous to soak up all the juices, it can be cooked either the night before or even in the morning, as it requires little input on your part.

Preheat the oven to 350°F. Slice the peppers in half, down the middle of the stalk. You should be left with four perfect sides. Remove the seeds and white flesh.

Lay the peppers cup side up on a baking tray and stuff with the cherry tomatoes (4 should fit perfectly in each pepper half), anchovies, and sliced garlic. Drizzle with olive oil and roast for 30 minutes. The peppers will fill with a delicious juice when cooking: take care not to let this escape when packing into your lunch receptacle!

COOKING THE NIGHT BEFORE: *Make in advance and leave early in the morning*

THAI FISHCAKES

Preparation time: 25 minutes. Makes 12 small fishcakes

- 2 x 7½ oz cans wild red or pink salmon
- 1 generous tbsp Thai red curry paste
- 1 tbsp fish sauce
- 1 egg, beaten
- pinch of salt
- all-purpose flour, as needed
- 3 scallions, very finely chopped
- 1 small red chili, seeded and finely chopped
- vegetable oil, for frying

For the cucumber salad
- splash of rice vinegar
- tiny splash of fish sauce
- ¼ red onion, very finely diced
- 1 tsp sweet chili sauce
- pinch of salt
- large pinch of sugar
- ⅓ small red chili, seeded and chopped
- ½ cucumber, halved lengthwise, seeded, and sliced into ¼ in thick crescents

R*ather than making these in advance for the sole purpose of eating them for your lunch the next day, why not make enough for that evening and for your lunch? This recipe will make enough for two people as a pre-dinner snack after a long and taxing day, and one person for lunch the following day. Just don't ruin your pre-planning skills by eating them all straight away*

The night before
Drain the salmon and add to a bowl, removing any skin and bones. Add the curry paste, fish sauce, beaten egg, and salt and mix thoroughly, until everything is well combined. You want a mixture that is thick enough to handle and form into patties, so if it's looking too wet add a bit of flour. Add the scallions and chopped chili and mix again. Separate the mix into little cakes, about 3 in wide, and put to the side on a plate. Heat about an inch of vegetable oil in a heavy-bottomed pan.

While the oil is heating, add everything for the cucumber salad dressing except the chili to a bowl and mix. Add the chili sparingly, and taste as you go for hotness. Keep the dressing and sliced cucumber separately in the fridge.

When the oil is very hot (you can test by dropping in a small piece of the fish mixture and seeing if it sizzles), carefully add the fishcakes and cook until crisp and brown on each side, around 2 minutes. Try not to over-handle them. Once cooked, remove and leave to sit on a plate covered with a paper towel. Enjoy piping hot as a pre-dinner treat with sweet chili sauce.

Come lunchtime
Refrigerate overnight and eat the leftovers the next day with the cucumber salad (mix the dressing and sliced cucumber together in a container in the morning). Try to keep everything refrigerated at work, if possible.

STUFFED EGGPLANT

Preparation time: 5 minutes, plus 35 minutes cooking
Makes 1 serving

- *1 large eggplant*
- *extra-virgin olive oil*
- *handful of fresh parsley (or any other green fresh herb you have to hand)*

- *2 good-quality sausages*
- *salt and freshly ground black pepper*

This dish is so flavorful that you might feel some kind of cultural obligation to have something bland alongside it to neuter it. If you must, couscous does the trick.

Preheat the oven on to 400°F. Slice the eggplant in half, down the middle of the stalk. Using a spoon, scoop out some of the flesh leaving at least ½ in thickness in the "shell." Drizzle some olive oil and a little salt over the hollowed eggplant halves.

Next, finely chop the scooped-out flesh along with the parsley and mix together in a bowl. Squeeze the sausage meat out of its skin and, using your hands, mix with the chopped eggplant and parsley. Divide the mixture between the 2 hollow eggplant halves and grind over some

black pepper. Place on a baking tray in the center of the oven and cook for 35 minutes.

Remove from the oven and leave to cool before putting in a container and popping in the fridge.

In the morning
Take to work and leave it at room temperature until you are ready to eat it. As previously indicated, couscous or a tomato and cucumber side salad could be nice here.

COOKING THE NIGHT BEFORE: *Make in advance and leave early in the morning*

CHICKPEA, CHORIZO & RED ONION
SCOTCH EGGS

....

Preparation time: 20 minutes, plus 25 minutes cooking. Makes 3—you could make just 1, but it would be a lot of effort. Any leftovers will keep for a day in the fridge—and what could be more cheering than coming home to a spare Scotch egg?

- 2½ in piece of dried chorizo, skinned and diced very finely
- ⅓ red onion, chopped
- 4 large eggs
- 2 x 15 oz can chickpeas, drained
- 4 tbsp extra-virgin olive oil
- salt and freshly ground black pepper

- 1 tsp paprika
- ¼ tsp chili flakes
- generous squirt of ketchup
- 1½ cups panko or regular breadcrumbs
- 1 tbsp all-purpose flour
- vegetable oil, for frying

....

There is no denying that this is more of a labor of love than most of the other recipes in this book, but these really are worth making as a treat. The most intimidating thing about making your own Scotch eggs, apart from the presence of scalding oil (and we would recommend that you make these the evening before, as deep-frying first thing in the morning is a bit stressful) is gauging whether the meat is cooked through. Luckily, you don't have to worry about that here.

....

The night before

Fill a pot, large enough to hold 3 eggs, with cold water and put on to boil. Put a small pan on a medium heat and, once hot, add the chorizo and onion (you don't need oil as the chorizo will release oil as it cooks). Leave for 5 minutes, stirring occasionally: you want everything to soften but not to crisp, so make sure to keep an eye on it. As soon as everything is nice and soft, turn the heat off.

Once the water is boiling, gently lower 3 eggs into it, setting your timer immediately for 6½ minutes. Turn up the heat if necessary: the water needs to remain at a steady, although not violent, boil. After 6½ minutes remove from the heat, drain the water, and run cold water over the eggs in the pot for 3 minutes.

Pour the chickpeas into the pan of chorizo and onion and place on a sturdy, heatproof surface. Begin to mash, using a potato masher, slowly adding the olive oil as you do so. The chickpeas should begin to break down and form a sort of mash, helped by the olive oil. When it has reached this consistency, season to taste, and add the paprika, chili, and a generous squirt of ketchup. Mix again. >

COOKING THE NIGHT BEFORE: *Make in advance and leave early in the morning*

You should be able to pick up a bit of mixture and squish it into a ball.

Fill two bowls: the first with breadcrumbs (add salt and pepper to these), and the other with the remaining egg, beaten. Pour the flour onto a clean plate. Your Scotch egg station is now ready.

Remove the eggs from the pot of cold water and carefully peel. It helps with the painful process of peeling if you do it under cold running water.

Take an 8 in piece of plastic wrap and place 2 large spoonfuls of the chickpea mix onto it. Mash this down with your hands, making sure that there are no holes. Place a peeled boiled egg on top and, using the plastic wrap like a blanket, wrap the chickpea mixture around it. Gently mold the chickpea mix around the egg, filling in any gaps with extra mix. Once you are happy with the shape (try to make it even, to help it fry evenly), roll in flour, then dip in beaten egg, and finally dip into the breadcrumb bowl. Make sure that the whole thing is evenly covered in breadcrumbs (you may have to pat them in). Place on a clean plate. Repeat this process for the two remaining eggs; you will need to wash your hands several times.

Add the oil to a large nonstick pan and heat until very hot. Test this by dropping a breadcrumb into the pan: if it sizzles and goes brown you're good to go. Carefully (and do be careful: it may sound obvious but burning oil, especially in the face, hurts) lower the Scotch eggs into the pan. Leave them to cook for approximately 40 seconds on each side, turning them with a spoon so that they are evenly cooked and golden brown all over. It is tempting to start doing the washing up now, but they burn really easily, so probably best to hold off. Once they are cooked, turn off the heat and remove from the pan with a slotted spoon, placing on a plate lined with a couple of pieces of paper towel. Leave to cool. If your eggs have suffered some casualties, don't worry too much. Just treat them like burnt toast and once it has cooled down a bit, gently scrape off any offending too-dark breadcrumbs.

In the morning
Line a Tupperware or lunch container with paper towel and add your egg (or eggs, if you've gone for two—and there is never any shame in going for two). A small jam jar of mayonnaise mixed with chili sauce is a good accompaniment—nestle into the Tupperware and refrigerate once you get to work.

COOKING THE NIGHT BEFORE: *Make in advance and leave early in the morning*

RATATOUILLE

Preparation time: 20 minutes frying, plus 30 minutes simmering
Makes 3 servings

- *plenty of extra-virgin olive oil*
- *1 onion, roughly chopped*
- *1 red pepper, sliced into chunks*
- *2 eggplants, chopped into chunks*
- *2 zucchini, chopped into chunks (and peeled if you wish)*
- *1 x 14½ oz can chopped tomatoes*
- *2 garlic cloves, crushed*
- *1 tsp dried thyme*
- *1 bay leaf*

You will need a large flameproof casserole dish and a large nonstick frying pan, along with a glass or two of red wine to keep you company as you cook this Provençal classic. What makes all the difference here is caramelizing the vegetables in stages, using the best extra-virgin olive oil you can afford, before adding them to the casserole for a final simmering.

Heat some olive oil in a frying pan, and soften the chopped onion and red pepper. Once these are cooked, transfer to the waiting casserole dish—on standby but not on the heat.

Next, drizzle 2 more tablespoons of olive oil into the frying pan and gently brown the eggplant, adding more olive oil if necessary to ensure the chunks don't stick to the pan and overcook.* When these are ready, add to the casserole and begin cooking the zucchini in the frying pan, again, adding olive oil if the pan looks too dry. Add to the casserole once ready.

Turn the heat on low under the casserole and stir in the chopped tomatoes, crushed garlic, thyme, and bay leaf. Leave to simmer for 30 minutes with the lid on. Then turn the heat off and leave to cool overnight.

In the morning
Help yourself to a portion of the ratatouille and put in a container. Slice a piece of crusty bread and carefully put it in a brown paper bag.

Come lunchtime
Ratatouille is delicious at room temperature, but you can of course reheat it if you wish. Enjoy with the bread, dipping it in the delicious sauce while humming the *Jean de Florette* theme tune.

* You could make extra eggplant here and put it aside for use in a day or two in the Falafel with yogurt, eggplant, and red cabbage salad (see page 40).

COOKING THE NIGHT BEFORE: *Make in advance and leave early in the morning*

PROVENÇAL TOMATOES

Preparation time: 5 minutes, plus 35 minutes cooking
Makes 1 serving

- 4 tomatoes
- 2 garlic cloves, crushed
- salt and freshly ground black pepper
- 1 tsp dried or 1 tbsp fresh basil, leaves torn

- breadcrumbs (optional)
- generous splash of extra-virgin olive oil
- ½ cup couscous

These are traditionally served at room temperature and are thus perfect for a packed lunch. The recipe calls for couscous, but these are also fantastic simply with crusty bread. So if your office happens to be near a bakery serving the finest bread rolls, perhaps indulge in one and use it to mop up the delicious juices.

Preheat the oven to 400°F. Cut each tomato into two even halves along its "equator" and place, cut side facing upward, on an ovenproof tray. Sprinkle the crushed garlic over the tomatoes along with the salt and pepper, basil, and the breadcrumbs, if using. Drizzle a generous amount of olive oil over the top and pop in the oven. Leave to cook for about 30–35 minutes. You want them nicely colored and charred in places, almost oozing.

Meanwhile, prepare the couscous in the container you're aiming to transport your lunch in. Simply pour in a generous amount of grains and cover with boiling water ¼ in over the top of the grains is usually enough. Cover with a dish towel and leave to plump. After a few minutes, separate using a fork.

When the tomatoes are ready, remove from the oven and immediately place them on the couscous, taking care to pour over all the lovely juices from the pan.

Leave on the countertop to cool overnight and to infuse.

Come lunchtime
Enjoy either reheated or at room temperature.

COOKING THE NIGHT BEFORE: *Make in advance and leave early in the morning*

QUICHE CRAIG-AINE

Preparation time: 1 hour
Makes 3 generous servings

- 2 tsp sunflower oil
- 1 onion, finely chopped
- 2 zucchini, peeled and sliced into ¼ in rounds
- salt and freshly ground black pepper
- 1 packet ready-rolled pie crust
- 3 eggs

- 1 tbsp freshly chopped parsley (optional)
- 3 tbsp cheese (feta or Gruyère work well)
- 1 heaped tbsp crème fraîche
- lettuce and tomato, to serve

Easy to transport, designed to be enjoyed at room temperature—what more need we say about quiche? Your colleagues will ask you where the new deli is, to which you'll reply, "Oh no. I made this."

Heat the oil in a frying pan on a medium to low heat, and add in the onion and zucchini. Sprinkle over some salt and cook until the zucchinis are golden and very soft—this should take about 25 minutes. Leave to cool on the side while you preheat the oven to 400°F.

Unroll the pastry. Line the base of an 8 in pie pan with parchment paper. Cover with the pastry, using your fingers to push it to the bottom of the dish. Using scissors, snip the excess round the edges until it looks nice and neat (using a rolling pin over the edges is also very effective). Poke the base with a fork to prevent it from rising up in the oven.

Crack the eggs into a bowl and whisk, adding salt and pepper, chopped parsley if using, cheese, and the crème fraîche.

Add the cooked zucchini to the pastry shell and cover with the egg mixture. Cook in the oven for 35–40 minutes, until the pastry is nice and golden.

When the quiche is cooked, leave to cool on the counter overnight, covered with aluminum foil.

In the morning
Prepare a mustard French dressing (see page 60) in a small jam jar, and pack a tomato and some lettuce in a container alongside a generous slice of your quiche. The remaining slices can of course be enjoyed for lunch the following day or, if you're feeling generous, given to your roommates.

Come lunchtime
Arrange your salad on a plate next to your quiche slice and pour over the dressing.

COOKING THE NIGHT BEFORE: *Make in advance and leave early in the morning*

TWO QUICKIE QUICHES

Preparation time: 5 minutes, plus 35–40 minutes cooking
Makes 3 generous servings

CLASSIC TUNA

- *3 eggs*
- *3 tbsp grated cheese (Gruyère or Cheddar)*
- *1 small can tuna, drained*
- *10 oz crème fraîche*
- *1 tbsp Dijon mustard*
- *1 tsp dried thyme*
- *freshly ground black pepper*

CLASSIC LORRAINE

- *3 eggs*
- *3 tbsp chopped bacon, gently fried in a little oil*
- *1 tbsp Dijon mustard*
- *3 tbsp grated cheese (Gruyère or Cheddar)*
- *10 oz crème fraîche*

These two classic quiches are both popular and labor-lite. Prepare the quiche pastry in a tin as with the Craig-aine and preheat the oven to 400°F. Then, simply beat all of the filling ingredients together with a fork in a bowl, and pour the mixture into the pastry. Cook for 35–40 minutes until the pastry is golden and the filling is set. Leave to cool on the counter overnight covered with foil.

COOKING THE NIGHT BEFORE: *Make in advance and leave early in the morning*

SPICY CHICKEN TAKEOUT

....

Preparation time: 5 minutes, plus 2 hours marinating and 35 minutes cooking
Makes 1 serving

- 2–3 chicken thighs, depending on appetite
- iceberg lettuce
- 1 bread roll

- 1 tsp garam masala
- 1 tsp paprika
- 1 tbsp extra-virgin olive oil

For the marinade
- 2 tbsp plain yogurt
- 1 in piece of fresh ginger, peeled and finely chopped
- 1 red chili, seeded and finely chopped

For the dip
- 2 tbsp plain yogurt
- squeeze of lemon juice
- salt and freshly ground black pepper
- 1 tbsp chopped fresh mint

....

There is no denying that this book has an overwhelming majority of vegetarian recipes. This is because, quite simply, meat is at its best when cooked and served immediately: the longer you leave it before eating, the tougher it gets. A sad picnicking truth. However, this little dish uses the tenderest part of the chicken coated in a protective layer of sauce, which helps it to stay tender for longer.

....

Score the chicken with a sharp knife down to the bone, and place in a bowl. Add all the marinade ingredients and mix together. Make sure you get the marinade right into the scored meat. Cover with plastic wrap and leave in the fridge for at least 2 hours.

Near the end of the marinating time, preheat the oven to 350°F. Remove the chicken from the fridge and place in an ovenproof dish. Bake for 35 minutes.

Leave to cool on the side while you prepare the yogurt dip. Combine all the ingredients in a Tupperware container and keep in the fridge. When the chicken has cooled, pop in a Tupperware alongside some iceberg lettuce. Leave in the fridge overnight.

In the morning
Pack your ingredients in your lunch conveyor along with the bread roll.

Come lunchtime
Leave your immediate desk area, and enjoy this takeout tribute with your fingers.

COOKING THE NIGHT BEFORE: *Make in advance and leave early in the morning*

6: GIVING LEFTOVERS A NEW LEASE ON LIFE

*S*ome things are best enjoyed on their first outing: stir fries spring to mind as being particularly impossible to revive the day after cooking, delicious though they are when just made. Similarly, rice doesn't really benefit from being returned to—who can eat leftover rice without fearing for their life? But there are other foodstuffs—a roast chicken, say—where the leftover potential is so great, so wide, so thrilling, that you want to roast the chicken on Sunday just to be able to make a soup with the scraps and bones on Monday. These are often our very favorite recipes, as they force you both to be creative and make a little go a long way.

CHICKEN, BASIL & AVOCADO COUSCOUS

Preparation time: 5 minutes
Makes 1 serving

- ½ avocado
- squeeze of lemon juice
- ½ cup couscous
- salt and freshly ground black pepper

- small handful of arugula
- 1 portion of leftover chicken, cut into fork-sized chunks
- generous handful of fresh basil

So simple and so delicious. This is more of an assembly job, as the avocado should be scooped out in spoonfuls just before serving and the only thing that needs cooking is the couscous.

In the morning

Put a pot of water on to boil. In a separated tiffin tin or lunch pail, gently place your avocado half in the top section and squeeze over some lemon juice to stop it going too brown before lunchtime. In the bottom section, pour in half a cupful of couscous and cover with the boiling water and a dish towel.

Once the couscous is ready and all the water has been absorbed, give it a fork through and season with salt and pepper. Top with the arugula and chicken chunks. Moisten two paper towels lightly and fold around the basil leaves and place in the top section with your avocado.

Come lunchtime

Scoop out the avocado flesh with a teaspoon and add to the couscous and chicken mix. Top with the basil leaves and stir.

REINVENTING LEFTOVERS: *Meat or fish that needs using up*

FAUX PHO

Preparation time: 15 minutes, plus 5 minutes assembly. Makes 1 serving

- 2 scallions, finely chopped
- 2 cups weak chicken stock, either homemade, ready prepared, or from a stock cube
- very small splash of fish sauce
- ½ lime
- handful of mint, leaves picked and washed
- handful of cilantro, leaves picked and washed
- handful of basil, washed and leaves torn
- large handful of leftover chicken, roughly pulled into pieces
- 1 portion of rice noodles
- ½ red chili
- Sriracha chili sauce (optional)

Wonderfully aromatic and light, this is a soup to both soothe and lift the spirits with all the essential flavors of pho and not so much of the fussing around. If you are in the lucky position of having leftovers from a whole roast chicken, then you could make your own stock for this, but store-bought stock or a bouillon cube works just fine. You'll need to have a few utensils waiting for you at your desk: a clean pair of scissors, a bowl, chopsticks, and a spoon.

In the morning

Fill your pot and put it on to boil. Add the chopped scallions to a nonstick pan on a low heat, and cook until they start to color. Put the stock in a pan on a medium heat, adding the fish sauce and the juice of a quarter of the lime. You want to heat it until just before it begins to boil, so while it is heating prepare your herbs and place in a container.

Place the chicken in a separate container, or wrap in a small piece of foil. Place the rice noodles in a large heatproof bowl, and pour over the boiling water. Cover with a clean dish towel and leave for 3 minutes. Remove the scallions from the heat and wrap in a small piece of foil. The stock should now be simmering, so turn off the heat and empty it into your thermos. Drain the noodles in a colander, shaking vigorously to get rid of any excess water and place in a Tupperware.

Come lunchtime

Find yourself a nice spot: this soup goes well with some quiet reflection. Carefully transfer your hot stock into a bowl, then add the noodles, chicken, and herbs. Lastly, using your scissors, snip the chili into the bowl, and squeeze the remaining quarter of lime juice generously. A squirt of chili sauce can be nice.

ASSEMBLE-AT-WORK LETTUCE LEAF WRAPS

Preparation time: 10 minutes, plus 5 minutes assembly
Makes 1 serving

- 3 scallions, chopped
- 12 raw shrimp (you could use a handful of leftover chicken/beef/pork instead of shrimp)
- small handful of mint leaves
- small handful of basil leaves
- 4 radishes, sliced
- 2 large iceberg lettuce leaves (discard the outermost leaves) washed and dried and torn in half, if using baby romaine use 4 leaves

For the dressing
- 1½ tbsp rice wine vinegar
- 1 tbsp sweet chili sauce
- ½ red chili, chopped

One of the most pleasing things about this recipe is how versatile it is: leftover scraps of chicken, beef, or shrimp all work well. Iceberg lettuce is best though—you want the lettuce leaves to be large-ish but firm and crunchy. Baby romaine would be a good alternative, although your wraps will be slightly smaller. Perfect for a lunch eaten on the grass on a sunny summer day.

In the morning
Put a pan on a high heat and add the scallions and shrimp. Cook for 4 minutes, then remove from the heat. While they're cooling, line a Tupperware with a piece of paper towel, then add the shrimp to it (or leftover meat if this is what you are using). Add your mint, basil, radishes, and lettuce leaves to a separate Tupperware, being careful not to break the lettuce.

Add the vinegar, chili sauce, and chopped chili to a clean jam jar and, checking the lid is securely fastened, give it a good shake to amalgamate.

Come lunchtime
Smugly get out your Tupperware. Using either your hands (make sure you have a few napkins) or actual cutlery if you have it, add 6 (or 3 if using baby romaine) shrimp, some charred scallions, radish slices, and herbs into the curved middle of the leaf, taking care not to overload it, then drizzle a splash of dressing over the top. Fold either side of the bare leaf over the middle, so that you make a sort of lettuce fajita, and eat immediately before the dressing escapes and drips all over you. Repeat until everything is used up.

COOKING THE NIGHT BEFORE: Meat or fish that needs using up

THE DELUXE

Preparation time: 25 minutes
Makes 1 serving

- 1 frozen baguette
- 1 tsp extra-virgin olive oil
- 3 (at least) slices of smoked bacon
- 1 chicken breast
- ½ avocado (very ripe)
- ½ lemon
- 1 tbsp mayonnaise
- salt and freshly ground black pepper

This is our attempt at recreating a sandwich enjoyed many years ago in an unassuming little French café on Bute Street in London. It was, in all probability, made with homemade bread and fresh mayonnaise, but we think our version holds its own nicely with Hellmann's and the ever-ready frozen baguette.

If you are using leftover cooked chicken, about a handful will probably suffice. Otherwise, we've included instructions below for poaching the chicken breast. We make this in the morning, however if you're likely to be short of time, make the filling the night before and simply bake your frozen baguette first thing.

Preheat the oven to 400°F and remove the baguette from the freezer. Fill a pot with salted water and put a lid on to bring to a boil.

Put a frying pan on a medium heat and add the oil. When hot, add the bacon and fry until it's just starting to go crispy. Turn the heat off and leave the bacon to cool before patting dry with paper towel. Then, using a pair of kitchen scissors, snip into small bite-sized pieces and pop in a mixing bowl.

By now, the oven should be hot. Put in the baguette and bake according to the package instructions, usually about 8–12 minutes. The pot of water should also be bubbling—turn the heat down to a gentle simmer, and add the chicken breast to the liquid. Leave to poach for 15 minutes.

Meanwhile, take your avocado half and, using a teaspoon, scoop out the lovely flesh, and add to the mixing bowl. Squeeze over a little lemon juice for now to stop it going brown.

If your baguette is looking golden brown, remove from the oven and leave to cool on the side.

Remove the chicken breast from the water after 15 minutes. If you're worried it feels a bit too floppy, slice it open in the thickest part and look to check it's not pink. If it needs a little more time, return to the hot water and put a lid on the pan. Don't put the heat back on

COOKING THE NIGHT BEFORE: *Meat or fish that needs using up*

otherwise the chicken will go too tough. Simply leave it in the hot water for 4 or 5 more minutes and all will be well.

When the chicken is cooked, leave to cool (or run under the cold tap and pat dry using a paper towel if you're in a hurry) before slicing thinly and adding to the mixing bowl. Add the spoonful of mayonnaise, some salt and freshly ground black pepper, and another generous squeeze of lemon before giving everything a good stir. Taste to check the seasoning before spreading inside your baguette. Pack tightly in foil.

If you're anywhere near as disorganized as us in life and find yourself lumbered with six packages of chicken breast expiring the next day, try poaching the lot in a pan of simmering water and keeping it in the fridge over the next few days for use in sandwiches and salads.

HARISSA CHICKEN SANDWICH

Preparation time: 25 minutes (including 15 minutes bread baking time)
Makes 1 serving

- 1 crusty roll, or a frozen baguette or frozen ciabatta
- large handful of leftover chicken meat
- 2 tbsp crème fraîche (if you don't have crème fraîche, mayonnaise works well too)
- 1 tsp harissa paste
- squeeze of lemon juice
- salt and freshly ground black pepper

A *fine way to finish a roast chicken's life.*

If you need to cook your bread, preheat the oven to 400°F. Put the chicken, crème fraîche, harissa, and lemon juice in a bowl and mix until everything has combined. Taste and season accordingly. Bake the bread in the oven for 12–15 minutes. You want it to be golden and crispy—this way you avoid the dreaded sog that is the peril of having a mayo-heavy filling.

While it's cooking, have a shower or get ready. Once cooked, remove the bread and leave to cool. Slice in half, leaving a hinge, and fill with the chicken mix. Wrap tightly in foil or parchment paper (if the latter, secure with string) and try not to open it before lunch.

COOKING THE NIGHT BEFORE: *Meat or fish that needs using up*

THE LONE SAUSAGE

Nothing harbors more potential than the lone sausage. Occasionally, you may have one left over from the previous night's sausage and mashed potatoes, or from a weekend breakfast's sausage sandwich, and your very understandable impulse is to just dunk it in some mustard and be done with it. Well, you could do that (and there is no denying that sometimes it is the only thing to do), but you could also make one of these simple recipes and really make the most of it.

LONE SAUSAGE CREAMY CHILI PASTA

Preparation time: 30 minutes
Makes 1 generous serving

- 2 tbsp extra-virgin olive oil
- 1 cooked sausage, split lengthwise and then diced
- ½ tsp dried chili flakes

- ½ x 14 oz can chopped tomatoes
- 2½ oz pasta of your choice
- 2 tbsp sour cream or crème fraîche
- salt and freshly ground black pepper

You'd never guess this recipe only uses one sausage. Creamy, spicy, and tasty—what's not to like?

First things first: put a pot of salted water on to boil. Add the oil to another pan and when warm, add the chopped sausage and chili flakes. Stir until the chili has had a chance to infuse the oil, then add the chopped tomatoes. Stir again and mash the tomatoes roughly with a potato masher, just to help them break down a bit.

Once the water is boiling, add the pasta. Add the sour cream to the tomatoey sauce and stir—it should combine smoothly; season to taste. Once the pasta is cooked, scoop out half a mugful of the cooking water before draining. Add both the pasta and the water to the sauce and mix thoroughly. Check the seasoning again and then transfer to a Tupperware.

LONE SAUSAGE WITH
CANNELLINI BEANS & TOMATOES

Preparation time: 10 minutes
Makes 1 serving

- 1 large tomato, chopped
- ¼ red onion, very finely chopped
- ½ garlic clove, very finely chopped
- 1 cooked sausage, split lengthwise and then diced
- ½ x 15 oz can of cannellini beans, drained

- 2 tbsp extra-virgin olive oil
- splash of red wine vinegar
- small handful of basil leaves
- salt and freshly ground black pepper

- piece of crusty bread, for juice mopping

*B*y all means use dried beans if you prefer, but we find the soaking a bit of a bother. Fresh beans are the nicest but hard to find, so we like to keep a stock of canned beans. Do try and buy good-quality ones—it does make a difference. No one likes a soggy bean.

In the morning
Combine all your ingredients in your lunch container and mix thoroughly, checking the seasoning. Make sure there's enough juice for mopping up. If there isn't, add a splash more oil and vinegar. Refrigerate once you get to work—this will benefit from sitting for a few hours while all the flavors get to know each other.

Come lunchtime
A slice of bread or a roll would be a good accompaniment.

LONE SAUSAGE WITH LENTILS

Preparation time: 35 minutes
Makes 1 serving

- 3½ oz dried lentils
- 1 stick of celery
- 1 garlic clove
- 1 tbsp extra-virgin olive oil

- salt and freshly ground black pepper
- 1 cooked sausage, thinly sliced
- piece of crusty bread or a slice of toast

A Continental take on the lone sausage. The lentils take a while to cook, so make this the night before then leave it sitting happily in the fridge overnight before transporting to work.

The night before

Put about ¾–1 cup water in a saucepan with the lentils, celery, and garlic and bring to a gentle boil. Simmer for 20 minutes, adding some salt after 10 minutes. Once cooked (the lentils should still be quite firm), drain thoroughly. Remove the celery and chop into small pieces. Add the lentils and celery to your lunch container, add the oil, mix and season, then add the sliced sausage and mix again.

Come lunchtime

A crusty bit of bread or a slice of toast is a good accompaniment for scooping up the lentils, and a side salad of lettuce and tomato with a simple oil and vinegar dressing makes this a very good lunch indeed.

A SIMPLE TORTILLA

Preparation time: 45 minutes
Makes 2 servings

- 2 tbsp extra-virgin olive oil
- 1 onion, halved and sliced into thin crescents
- 1 potato, halved and sliced into thin crescents
- salt and freshly ground black pepper

- 4 eggs
- 2 Laughing Cow triangles (optional but recommended)

Although not very labor-intensive, this takes some slow cooking, so it's not a recipe to embark on if you're rushed for time. If you have any other veg to hand, you can of course add it at the same time as the onions and potatoes.

Add the oil to a frying pan and, when hot, add the sliced onions and potatoes. Fry on a medium heat for 3 minutes, stirring frequently, until everything begins to brown. Turn the heat down to the very lowest setting, season with salt and pepper, and put a lid on the pan. Leave for 20 minutes to steam.

Crack the eggs into a bowl, whisk very lightly (don't worry about them being completely combined), and season with salt and pepper. If you have one of those welcome cheese fridge surprises on hand, such as a couple of Laughing Cow triangles, break them into the egg mixture.

Remove the onion and potatoes from the heat, then pour the egg mixture over. Return to a very low heat, covering the pan with a lid, and leave for 10 minutes. Finish off under a broiler for 5 minutes, then remove and leave to cool.

Slice in half and wrap one half securely in foil. A small salad is a nice accompaniment, but by no means necessary.

PEARL BARLEY WITH CARROTS

Preparation time: 5 minutes, plus 35 minutes cooking
Makes 2 servings

- 1 cup pearl barley
- 1 bay leaf
- 1 garlic clove
- 3 carrots, sliced diagonally into ¾ in chunks
- 2 red onions, quartered

- leaves from 3–4 sprigs thyme (or 1 tsp dried thyme)
- 1 tbsp extra-virgin olive oil
- salt and freshly ground black pepper
- 1 tsp cider vinegar

At home, we always seem to run out of gin and chocolate, but for some "inexplicable" reason, carrots and onions cling to our fridge drawers like barnacles. This dish uses these fridge stalwarts up nicely. You could, of course, trade the carrots for butternut squash or pumpkin if you've been afflicted with them in your veg box and, four weeks on, they're still more kitchen decoration than ingredient.

The night before

Preheat the oven to 350°F. Rinse the barley under the tap before adding to a saucepan with plenty of cold, salted water. Add the bay leaf and garlic clove and bring the lot to a gentle boil; simmer for 35 minutes.

While the barley is simmering, place the carrots and onions on a baking tray, and top with the thyme, olive oil, and salt and pepper. Roast for 30 minutes.

Drain the barley in a colander, and add to your lunch container. Drizzle over the cider vinegar and check the seasoning, adding more salt if necessary. Remove the carrots and onions from the oven and stir into the barley, along with any juices. Leave to cool on the countertop until the morning.

In the morning

Transport to work and, ideally, pop in a fridge on arrival. If eating at room temperature, remember to take out an hour before eating.

CARROT AND POPPY SEED SALAD
WITH RYE BREAD

Preparation time: 5 minutes
Makes 1 serving

- 2–3 slices rye bread (depending on appetite)
- 2 carrots
- a little freshly ground black pepper
- juice of ½ lemon
- 1 tsp poppy seeds
- 1 tbsp soft cheese (hummus also works well)

This is a simple, light lunch and, to be frank, barely a recipe. But sometimes we feel that in this world of delicious yet overcomplicated layered dishes, there is something beautiful about a simple meal of bread and cheese, with a little crunch alongside. The tomato salsa on page 55 would also be a nice accompaniment.

In the morning
Wrap the rye bread in foil or a brown paper bag and pack separately. Peel the carrots and trim the ends. Grate the carrot into your lunch container and add a little black pepper, the lemon juice, and poppy seeds. Mix well. Spoon the soft cheese (or hummus) into a small jam jar or mini Tupperware container, and nestle into the carrot salad.

Come lunchtime
Unwrap your rye and spread with the cheese or hummus. Pile the carrots on top and enjoy.

A WORD ON SOFT CHEESE
Soft cheeses like cream cheese work well, but Laughing Cow, no doubt controversially, is a truly fine choice: it comes in individual foil packages and can survive out of the fridge for several hours. It seems obvious to us that serious packed lunchers would lean toward the giggly bovine in their lunching adventures.

7: BRIBING COLLEAGUES WITH SWEET TREATS

In many ways, working in an office is not so different from being at school. There is the same unspoken rule that, when you go on vacation, even if that vacation is two days at home doing personal admin and catching up on box sets, you must bring back local candy for the enjoyment of your colleagues.

How many of us suffer the last-minute crazed scramble to purchase authentic Bulgarian plant-based boiled candy, rather than endure the shame of producing a duty-free mini Toblerone multipack, symptomatic of colleague neglect. It is a levy that you must pay for having dared to go away.

That said, there is nothing like giving your colleagues a bit of sugar to endear you to them. No one likes a creep, true, but sometimes it's nice to share the fruits of your weekend baking—and any excuse for a 4 p.m. break and cup of coffee is a good one.

SALTED CARAMEL BROWNIES

Preparation time: 20 minutes, plus 50 minutes cooking
Makes enough for all your colleagues and probably your roommates too

- 14 tablespoons unsalted butter, plus melted butter for greasing the pan
- 12¼ oz dark chocolate
- 4 eggs
- 1 lb superfine sugar
- scant ¾ cup all-purpose flour, sifted

For the salted caramel
- 5 tbsp unsalted butter
- ¼ cup light brown sugar
- ¼ cup superfine sugar
- ¼ cup golden syrup (or light corn syrup)
- ½ cup heavy cream
- 1 tsp Maldon sea salt

These are definitely worth the extra effort, with the excuse that it's a good opportunity to make extra salted caramel for pouring over ice cream, eating off your finger, etc., etc.

Preheat the oven to 350°F. Butter a 9 in square cake pan and line with parchment paper.

In a bain marie (a heatproof bowl placed over a very small amount of boiling water in a small pot), melt the chocolate and butter.

While this is melting, make your salted caramel. Put the butter, sugars, and golden syrup in a pan and place over a low heat until it melts. Leave to bubble gently for 4 minutes, stirring occasionally. Take off the heat and stir in the cream, then return to heat and cook for another 3 minutes. Take off the heat again and add the sea salt. Taste (making sure that it is cool enough first) and add more salt if necessary. Leave to one side.

Using an electric hand whisk if you have one, or an ordinary whisk if you don't,

beat the eggs and sugar until they are creamy and shiny. Gently mix in the melted chocolate and butter mixture and then fold in the sifted flour. Drizzle a third of the caramel mix in, mixing roughly so it is not fully combined. Spoon half the mix into the cake pan, drizzle on another third of caramel, then pour over the remaining brownie mix. Top with the last of the caramel and smooth with a knife. The caramel should be marbled throughout.

Bake for 50 minutes until the top is shiny and crispy. If you're not sure if the brownies are cooked, stick a sharp knife or toothpick in: if it comes out looking clean-ish then they are ready. Leave to cool.

Cut into small-ish squares and transport your spoils in a cake pan, or a Tupperware lined with parchment paper or paper towel.

BRIBING COLLEAGUES WITH SWEET TREATS: *When you really need some goodwill*

PACKING TIP

If you have more than one layer of brownie or cake, line each layer with some paper towel or parchment paper to prevent the squares from sticking together.

PEANUT BUTTER & JELLY BROWNIES

Preparation time: 10 minutes, plus 50 minutes cooking
Makes about 20 squares (depending on how large you slice them)

- 12¼ oz dark chocolate
- 14 tbsp unsalted butter, plus melted butter for greasing the pan
- 4 eggs
- 2 cups superfine sugar
- scant ¾ cup all-purpose flour, sifted

- 1 small packet salted peanuts
- 4 generous tbsp peanut butter—you can use either smooth or crunchy, though you may wish to adjust the quantity of peanuts accordingly
- 5 generous tbsp jam

These deliciously salty and sweet brownies are a nod to the great American packed lunch staple that is the peanut butter and jelly sandwich. You can add many things to a brownie mix, as we have discovered, but jelly is not one of them. We like to use a cherry or raspberry jam or preserves, although any seedless red fruit jam should work well.

Preheat the oven to 350°F. Butter a 9 in square cake pan and line with parchment paper.

In a bain marie (a heatproof bowl placed over a very small amount of boiling water in a small pan), melt the chocolate and butter.

While this is melting, beat the eggs and sugar until they are creamy and shiny—use an electric hand whisk if you have one, or an ordinary whisk if you don't.

Once the chocolate and butter have melted completely, remove the bowl from the heat and leave to cool. Gently mix the chocolate and butter mixture into the eggs and sugar, adding it bit by bit, and then fold in the sifted flour.

Add the peanuts and mix thoroughly, then add 2 tablespoons of peanut butter, mixing in roughly so that it does not fully combine with the brownie mix. Spoon the mixture into your prepared cake pan. This is where you can be artistic and have some fun: blob the jam and remaining spoons of peanut butter onto the mixture, and swirl in and around with a knife. You want both the jam and peanut butter to be layered throughout and well distributed. Smooth the top with a knife: the surface should look lovely and marbled.

Bake for 50 minutes until the top is shiny and crispy. If you're not sure if the brownies are cooked, stick a sharp knife or toothpick in: if it comes out looking clean-ish, then they are ready. Leave to cool. See pages 184–5 for transportation tips.

BRIBING COLLEAGUES WITH SWEET TREATS: *When you really need some goodwill*

QUEEN CAKES

Preparation time: 10 minutes, plus 20–30 minutes cooking
Makes 12 cakes

- *scant ½ cup superfine sugar*
- *1 tbsp unsalted butter, softened*
- *scant ¾ cup self-rising flour*

- *2 eggs*
- *1¾ oz golden rasins*
- *confectioners' sugar, to dust*

*D*elightfully simple, and with the usually ubiquitous ton of buttery frosting absent, these little cakes are hard to resist. Your team meeting won't be the same again.

Preheat the oven to 350°F and line a 12-hole muffin tin with cupcake papers. Put all of the ingredients (except the raisins and confectioners' sugar) in a large bowl and mix together using a wooden spoon until everything is combined and there are no lumps. Stir in the raisins.

Spoon the mixture into the paper cases and bake in the oven for 20–30 minutes, until the tops are golden and springy to the touch. Leave to cool before dusting over a little confectioners' sugar using a sieve.

LEMON CURD CUPCAKES

Preparation time: 15 minutes, plus 15 minutes cooking and 10 minutes to cool
Makes 12—or 10 if you find it hard not to eat raw batter

- *¼ cup superfine sugar*
- *1 stick unsalted butter, softened*
- *1 cup self-rising flour*
- *2 eggs*

- *finely grated zest of 1 lemon*
- *squeeze of lemon juice*
- *⅓ jar of lemon curd*
- *confectioners' sugar, to dust*

These are so simple to make that you can easily knock them out in half an hour in between TV watching on a Sunday evening.

Preheat your oven to 400°F. Put the sugar in a large bowl, then add the butter in small chunks, mixing vigorously until combined. Sift in the flour, add the eggs, and combine. Add the lemon zest and squeeze of lemon juice and mix.

Lay the cupcake papers in a muffin tin and spoon a small teaspoonful of the mix into them. Using the end of a teaspoon dig a little well in the center of each, and add half a teaspoonful of lemon curd. Top with one more small teaspoonful of cupcake batter, and smooth over so the curd is all covered. Repeat until they're all done (try not to eat too much batter as you go along—it will make you feel sick) and bake for 15 minutes, or until pale golden brown. Leave to cool for 10 minutes and then dust with confectioners' sugar. Take to work and enjoy peoples' surprise as they take a bite and discover the hidden lemon curd.

CUPBOARD CHOC CHIP COOKIES

Preparation time: 15 minutes, plus 10 minutes cooking
Makes about 15

- 5 tbsp salted butter, softened
- 3 tbsp light brown sugar
- ¼ cup granulated sugar
- 1 tsp vanilla extract
- 1 egg

- 1 scant cup all-purpose flour
- ½ tsp baking soda
- ¼ tsp sea salt
- 3½ oz chocolate chunks of your choice
- 1 tbsp cocoa powder (optional)

Whether it's as an after-dinner treat or a 4 p.m. snack with a cup of coffee or tea, who can say no to a cookie? What's more, it's easy to make them with ingredients you already have in the kitchen cabinet. Regular chocolate chip is a classic, but it can be fun to use novelty chocolates like M&M's, or, for a classier treat, butterscotch or toffee chocolate bars. Or whatever else you have lying around. For a double choc chip effect, just add a tablespoon of cocoa powder at the same time as the flour.

Preheat the oven to 350°F. In a large bowl beat the butter and sugars together until combined. Add the vanilla extract and the egg, and mix together well.

Sift the flour and baking soda slowly into the butter and sugar, and mix until it comes together into a dough. Add the salt and chocolate chunks (and the cocoa powder, if using) and mix well. Line two baking trays with parchment paper, and use a teaspoon to divide the mixture into small balls. Space them well apart, squashing each ball down a bit as you lay it out. Bake for around 10 minutes—they should be golden brown and still a bit soft in the middle. Swat any grasping hands away, and transfer to a tin or Tupperware lined with parchment paper—that is if you have any of them left to take into work the next day.

CHOCOLATE FRIDGE "CRACK" BARS

....

Preparation time: 20 minutes, then leave to chill overnight
Makes more than enough to share

- 9 oz digestive cookies (or graham crackers)
- 3½ oz dark chocolate
- 9 oz fruit and nut chocolate
- 1 tbsp unsalted butter

- 3 large tbsp golden syrup (or light corn syrup)
- handful of nuts (optional)
- handful golden raisins/other dried fruit (optional)
- ½ tsp sea salt

....

R*efined they are not, but these little bars have a lot of other things going for them:
you don't have to bake them, you can buy all the ingredients from the corner store,
they're cheap and quick to make . . . just be warned that they are fiendishly addictive.*

....

L ine a large Tupperware or a small, deep baking tray or rectangular baking dish (approx 6" x 8") with plastic wrap. Empty the cookies into a (clean) plastic bag and crush with a rolling pin or can (you want chunks not powder, so don't go mad).

In a bain marie (a heatproof bowl placed over a very small amount of boiling water in a small pan), melt both types of chocolate, butter, and golden syrup.

Once melted, remove from the heat, stir in the crushed cookies, and add nuts/raisins/salt as you wish. Stir well so that everything is combined, then spoon into your plastic-lined container.

Leave to cool in the fridge overnight, then turn out onto a cutting board. Remove the plastic wrap and cut into pieces with a sharp knife. Take to work and smugly produce your tin of treats at the 4 p.m. coffee break.

BRIBING COLLEAGUES WITH SWEET TREATS: *Baking cupcakes like a girl*

PLANNING AHEAD:
WEEKLY MENUS AND SHOPPING LISTS

....

*I*t's easy to have the best intentions when it comes to making your lunch, especially at the beginning of the week (actually, this applies to most things). But even the most enthusiastic of lunch makers—ourselves included—can lack inspiration at times. Who hasn't left work late and a bit frazzled and, stopping off at the store on the way home to pick up groceries, returned with a pack of chocolate, a gallon of milk, and some broccoli? On nights like these it's difficult enough to decide what you're going to make for dinner, let alone lunch. Of course we've already extolled the virtues of keeping a few basics in your kitchen cabinet, but thinking about what you might want to make before going shopping can also be very useful (and cut down on the time you spend wandering aimlessly around your local supermarket in a zombie-like trance). Planning—even loosely—in advance cuts down on waste too. How often do you buy a bunch of cilantro for a specific recipe, and then find the remnants molding, forgotten, at the bottom of the fridge a few days later?

....

*B*earing all this in mind, we've prepared a few weekly shopping lists with suggestions for weekday lunch recipes. The recipes selected share shopping ingredients but are also varied, as no matter how much you might love cabbage, no one wants to eat it every day. We've also suggested the optimum time for preparing the dishes.

1: VEGETARIAN

This book isn't short of vegetarian recipes, but this weekly plan is a good mix of textures and flavors.

SHOPPING LIST
Black beans
Bok choi (Chinese cabbage)
Black olives
Cheese
Chili
Cilantro
Eggs
Laughing Cow cheese triangles
Limes
Mayonnaise
Noodles
Onions
Parmesan
Potatoes
Puff pastry
Scallions
Sweet corn

Monday
Morning: Mexican-style corn

Tuesday
Morning / evening before:
Black bean soup

Wednesday
Morning: Done-up instant noodles

Thursday
Morning / evening before:
Pissaladière (minus the anchovies)

Friday
Morning / evening before:
A simple tortilla

2: "EXOTIC"

Maybe it's overexposure to the national treasure that is the sandwich, but sometimes you just fancy eating things that are a bit fresh or spicy, and that haven't been stuffed between two slices of whole wheat bread.

SHOPPING LIST
Cabbage
Carrots
Chicken
Chickpeas
Chilies
Cilantro
Cucumber
Curry paste
Lettuce
Lemons
Limes
Mint
Radishes
Canned salmon
Scallions
Tomatoes

Monday
Morning: Faux pho (use Sunday's leftover chicken)
Evening: Thai fishcakes

Tuesday
Morning: Thai fishcakes (leftover from the evening before) and Vietnamese salad

Wednesday
Morning: Chickpea salad with cumin

Thursday
Morning: Tabouleh

Friday
Morning: Assemble-at-work lettuce leaf wraps (using leftover meat from the evening before)

3: HEALTHY

Healthy doesn't have to be boring: add spice or beans to jazz things up a bit, and give yourself a treat on Friday.

SHOPPING LIST
Anchovies
Avocado
Black olives
Cannellini beans
Chickpeas
Crème fraîche
Carrots
Cilantro
Cucumber
Eggs
Eggplant
Falafels
Green beans
Lettuce
Limes
Red cabbage
Red onion
Salad ingredients
Tomatoes
Canned tuna
Yogurt

Monday
Morning: Salad Niçoise with a boiled egg in its shell

Tuesday
Morning: Cannellini bean and tuna salad

Wednesday
Morning: Avocado salad

Thursday
Morning: Rainbow rescue

Friday
The evening before: Falafel with yogurt, eggplant and red cabbage salad (use remaining cilantro and substitute crème fraîche for yogurt)

4: WHEN WINTER SUSTENANCE IS NEEDED

Winter tends to mean more evenings in, so cooking the night before makes sense, and is less of a sacrifice than when the beer garden and friends are calling. The key here is things you can reheat—and carbs, of course.

SHOPPING LIST
Anchovies
Bread
Capers
Chorizo
Couscous
Lima beans
Lone sausage
Olives
Pasta
Red peppers
Sour cream
Canned tomatoes
Fresh tomatoes

Monday
The evening before: Chorizo and lima bean stew-ette

Tuesday
The evening before: Puttanesca (ideally left over from Monday's dinner, so you only need cook once)

Wednesday
The evening before: Roasted red peppers with anchovy and tomato

Thursday
Morning (but you could roast your peppers and tomatoes in advance when you roast the peppers)
Chorizo with couscous, roasted peppers, and tomatoes

Friday
Morning: Lone sausage creamy chili pasta

5: THRIFTY LUNCHES FOR THE WEEK BEFORE PAYDAY

This is all about rummaging, making the most of what you've already got, and buying as few additional ingredients as possible.

SHOPPING LIST
Canned black beans
Bok choi (Chinese cabbage)
Chilies
Cilantro
Couscous
Eggs
Feta cheese
Frozen peas
Instant noodles
Lemons
Limes
Mint
Onions
Scallions
Tomatoes

Monday
Morning: Quick couscous version of Herby quinoa with peas

Tuesday
The evening before:
Pea and mint soup

Wednesday
Morning: Done-up instant noodles

Thursday
The evening before: Black bean soup

Friday
Morning or the evening before: Pea, feta, and chili frittata or, if you've reached your pea limit, Tomato couscous

6: THE MINIMUM OF FUSS

Quick, easy recipes for those weeks where you don't have enough time and it feels like you only go home to sleep and eat.

SHOPPING LIST
Avocados
Bacon
Basil
Cannellini beans
Capers
Couscous
Cucumber
Frozen peas
Lettuce
Mint
Parsley
Pita
Sourdough
Canned tuna
Tomatoes

Monday
Morning: Avocado salad in a pita

Tuesday
Morning: Quick couscous version of Herby quinoa with peas

Wednesday
Morning: Tuna with basil and capers in a pita

Thursday
The evening before: Cannellini bean and tuna salad

Friday
Morning (but cook the bacon the night before for maximum speed): BALT sourdough sandwich

7: MEDITERRANEAN STYLE

This plan is best enjoyed in the summer, during the Mediterranean vegetable apogee.

SHOPPING LIST
Chickpeas
Cucumber
Eggplant
Falafel
Lemons and limes
Mint
Parsley
Peppers
Red cabbage
Red onions
Tomatoes
Yogurt
Zucchini

Monday
The night before: Ratatouille (fry extra eggplant for Tuesday's falafel)

Tuesday
Morning: Falafel with yogurt, eggplant and red cabbage salad (bake the falafel for 10 minutes in the oven while you chop the veg and prepare the dressing)

Wednesday
Morning: Roasted vegetable tart, using leftover ratatouille (see page 133, after Tomato, pesto, and goat cheese tart)

Thursday
Morning: Tabouleh

Friday
Morning: Spicy chickpea dip

8: EMBRACING AL FRESCO LUNCHING

For that summer heatwave.

SHOPPING LIST
Avocado
Basil
Carrots
Cherry tomatoes
Chickpeas
Cilantro
Cucumber
Green beans
Halloumi
Smoked herring
Lettuce
Lime
Red cabbage
Red onions
Red peppers

Monday
Morning: Chickpea, Parmesan, and red onion salad

Tuesday
In the morning (if you have time) or the evening before: Grilled halloumi, vegetable, and avocado couscous

Wednesday
Morning: Rainbow rescue

Thursday
Morning: Avocado salad

Friday
Morning: Simple guacamole and tomato salsa on rye

INDEX

ABOUT THE AUTHORS

SOPHIE MISSING *grew up in London and studied English at UCL. She worked in publishing for four years, where she edited lots of delicious cookbooks. She now works as a freelance writer, editor, and occasional food stylist—but still makes a lot of packed lunches.*

CAROLINE CRAIG *grew up in London but comes from a family of fruit farmers and wine producers. A childhood spent gobbling home-grown black truffles, tomatoes, and peaches left her with little choice but to shape her life around food and entertaining. Caroline writes a column for* The Guardian *with co-author Sophie Missing, and works at the Royal Botanic Gardens.*

ACKNOWLEDGMENTS

It takes a lot of work and enthusiasm to make a book, and we are very grateful to everyone who has encouraged and helped us along the way. Bearing this in mind, here is our Oscar acceptance speech . . . we mean, book acknowledgments.

Thank you to:
David Loftus, for taking such unbelievably brilliant photos and making our packed lunches look so good.

Simon Josebury for doing a perfect job on the design.

Jon Elek, our agent and the Ari Gold of the literary world, for being generally wonderful, and a mean sandwich maker.

Tim Sandford, who never fails to forget his packed lunch in the fridge at home.

Our colleagues at Penguin UK, especially Juliet Annan, Will Hammond, Matt Clacher (unofficial author photographer), and John Hamilton for advice, title suggestions and generally being kind and supportive. Special mention to Jenny Fry, Tamsin English, and Jo Wickham.

Ed Griffiths; Laura Hassan; Tom Fleming ("pack it up, pack it in"); Craig Taylor; Josephine Maxwell (sorry we couldn't call your recipe by its real name: SLOP); Nathalie Dubant for making Caroline dozens of BLTs over the years; Lucy Buglass for the bacon lattice; Holly and Sue Morgan for countless special sandwiches; Jen Liscio for Orzo pasta salad inspiration; Poppy North for the weird and wonderful combo that is hummus and salami; Sara Batmanglich for making Sophie Mexican corn for the first time.

Friends we have lived with and cooked with and who have often cooked for us over the years: Etta Howells, Tom Bennett, Frank Carson, Ellen Parr, Hannah Daniel, Susannah Webb, Georgia Lee, Carolanne Dubant, David Alty, Chloe Tapp, Greg Kyle-Langley.

Francoise Craig, Richard Craig, who instilled their thrifty packed lunch ways in Caroline from birth; Sara Craig and Estelle Craig for being wonderful sisters.

Paul Missing, chickpea maestro; Debbie Missing, luxe packed lunch queen; Jake Missing, exacting consumer of lunches and only somewhat reluctant washer-upper. Thank you for letting us wreak havoc in your kitchen.